D1552548

INTERPERSONAL PSYCHOTHERAPY FOR DYSTHYMIC DISORDER

INTERPERSONAL PSYCHOTHERAPY FOR DYSTHYMIC DISORDER

JoHN C. MARKOWITZ, M.D.
Associate Professor of Clinical Psychiatry
Cornell University Medical College
Director, Psychotherapy Clinic
Payne Whitney Clinic
New York Hospital
New York, New York

Washington, DC
London, England

Note: The author has worked to ensure that all information in this book concerning drug dosages, schedules, and routes of administration is accurate as of the time of publication and consistent with standards set by the U.S. Food and Drug Administration and the general medical community. As medical research and practice advance, however, therapeutic standards may change. For this reason and because human and mechanical errors sometimes occur, we recommend that readers follow the advice of a physician who is directly involved in their care or the care of a member of their family.

Books published by the American Psychiatric Press, Inc., represent the views and opinions of the individual authors and do not necessarily represent the policies and opinions of the Press or the American Psychiatric Association.

Copyright © 1998 American Psychiatric Press, Inc.
ALL RIGHTS RESERVED
Manufactured in the United States of America on acid-free paper
First Edition   01   00   99   98   4   3   2   1
American Psychiatric Press, Inc.
1400 K Street, N.W., Washington, DC   20005

Library of Congress Cataloging-in-Publication Data

Markowitz, John C., 1954–
    Interpersonal psychotherapy for dysthymic disorder / John C.
Markowitz.
        p.   cm.
    To be used in conjunction with: Interpersonal psychotherapy of
depression / Gerald L. Klerman . . . [et al.]. c1984.
    Includes bibliographical references and index.
    ISBN 0-88048-914-6
    1. Depression, Mental—Treatment.   2. Psychotherapy.
3. Psychotherapist and patient.   I. Interpersonal psychotherapy of
depression.   II. Title.
    [DNLM: 1. Dysthymic Disorder—therapy.   2. Psychotherapy—methods.
3. Interpersonal Relations.   4. Randomized Controlled Trials.
5. Antidepressive Agents—therapeutic use.   WM 171 M346i 1998]
RC537.M359   1998
616.85′270651—dc21
DNLM/DLC
for Library of Congress   97-25436
                                                                            CIP

British Library Cataloguing in Publication Data
A CIP record is available from the British Library.

In grateful appreciation of my mentors:
the late Gerald L. Klerman, M.D.,
who taught me IPT;
James H. Kocsis, M.D.,
who taught me about chronic depression;
and the late Samuel W. Perry, M.D.,
who with the other two pushed me ahead in research.
And to my wife, colleague, and proofreader
Kathleen Clougherty, A.C.S.W.,
who helped in all spheres.
All have given me great guidance.

—J.C.M.

CONTENTS

ACKNOWLEDGMENTS

My great thanks to Myrna M. Weissman, Ph.D., who took over as an IPT mentor when Gerry Klerman died and who has provided unstinting support ever since. To Jack Barchas, M.D., a chairman who was most patient in awaiting my getting a grant. To a host of teachers and colleagues at Payne Whitney, including Stuart Asch, M.D., Michael Beldoch, Ph.D., Hyam Bolocan, M.D., Arnold M. Cooper, M.D., Bob Michels, M.D., Allen Frances, M.D., and Baruch Fishman, Ph.D., and to colleagues further afield, including A. John Rush, M.D. To Sabrina Cherry, M.D., Polly Scarvalone, Ph.D., Peter Shapiro, M.D., Holly Swartz, M.D., and many other supervisees who taught me more about IPT. To Kathy Dodd, Alyce Kuklinski, and Liliana Villalobos, who helped me get this manuscript out. To my parents, particularly my father, Joel Markowitz, M.D., who inculcated my interest in psychiatry. And to my daughter Caitlin, a constant inspiration and the world's youngest expert on IPT.

My time was supported in part by grants MH19069, MH46250, and MH49635 from the National Institute of Mental Health and from a fund established in The New York Community Trust by DeWitt-Wallace.

PREFACE

This book for mental health professionals is an outgrowth of a treatment manual developed primarily for research purposes. The late Gerald L. Klerman, M.D., and I wrote the manual to guide the training of psychotherapists and the conduct of an interpersonal psychotherapy treatment study of dysthymic disorder (IPT-D). I hope that it also will prove useful to other researchers and to clinicians.

This manual was designed at Cornell University Medical College for use in a randomized comparative treatment study of dysthymic disorder, which has received funding from the National Institute of Mental Health (R01-MH49635). This research will compare the relative efficacy of 1) IPT-D, 2) a form of supportive psychotherapy, and 3) the serotonin reuptake inhibiting antidepressant medication sertraline plus a manualized "clinical management" condition in treating dysthymic disorder of primary, early onset type. Sections of the manual describe in detail the adaptation of IPT to the treatment of dysthymic patients for this research project.

This book should be read in conjunction with the fuller description of interpersonal psychotherapy presented in the original IPT treatment manual by Klerman and colleagues (1984).

INTRODUCTION

The purpose of the book is to promote better understanding of a misunderstood syndrome, dysthymic disorder, and to delineate approaches to its treatment, particularly interpersonal psychotherapy (IPT; Klerman et al. 1984).

The idea for this book came from dysthymic patients. Within a brief span of time, two patients told me that they had looked up depression, one in a popular book, the other in a medical text. Both had been confused by what they found and did not find. Descriptions of depression tend to focus on the relatively brief, symptomatically severe syndrome called major depression and on manic depression, or bipolar disorder (American Psychiatric Association 1994). My patients had read about these but had seen no mention of their own condition.

It is hard to find descriptions of the insidious, lingering, chronic depression, the "walking" form of persistent misery now called dysthymic disorder. Dysthymic disorder is relatively recently defined but long widespread, misunderstood, and underreported. This book aims to explain dysthymic disorder to clinicians and also to "educated consumers," who may learn to recognize this disorder in themselves or those close to them and seek effective treatment.

This book focuses on IPT as a treatment for dysthymic disorder (IPT-D). IPT is an exciting therapy whose benefits have been demonstrated in the treatment of other forms of mood disorders and other psychiatric syndromes (Klerman and Weissman 1993). IPT may be learned from a book but is probably best assimilated—like most clinical techniques—through the additional training of supervision from a therapist certified in IPT. For a fuller discussion of IPT, readers are referred to the original IPT manual by Klerman, Weissman, Rounsaville, and Chevron: *Interpersonal Psychotherapy of Depression* (1984). Reading the current book may allow experienced psychotherapists to attempt IPT with dysthymic patients, albeit without supervision they may find it hard to generate the confidence necessary to work with such potentially discouraging patients as dysthymic individuals can appear. IPT is only one of several available psychological and pharmacological treatments for dysthymic disorder.

IPT-D will look more behavioral on the page than it should be in practice. In writing this, as in workshop presentations I have given, I am concerned that the description will sound too behavioral and mechanical. This may be an inherent difficulty of explaining a psychotherapeutic technique. Workshop participants have commented on the difference between the nuts and bolts description of IPT techniques, which can sound quite structured, and the freer form of the actual treatment evident in videotaped sessions and role-played simulations. The latter reflect what IPT should be; IPT has a structure, and guidelines to follow, but in practice is less confining than, for example, behavioral or cognitive behavioral treatments. For the psychodynamically trained practitioner IPT requires relatively little adjustment; in general the key changes are an increase in therapist activity, a medical model, a time-limited focus, and greater attention to the "here and now"—meaning outside, rather than within, sessions.

Psychotherapy research has entered an exciting phase. Researchers have shown that time-limited treatments can be designed to target particular psychiatric syndromes and that such treatments actually work. The application of IPT to dysthymic disorder is an exciting example of a time-limited therapy meeting a chronic and timeless disorder, with potentially dramatic results.

SECTION 1
Overview of Dysthymic Disorder

Dum anima est, spes est.
(While there's life, there's hope.)

—Marcus Tulius Cicero,
Ad Atticum

SECTION 1

Overview of Dysrhythmic Disorder

CHAPTER 1
Dysthymic Disorder

Canst thou not minister to a mind diseased,
Pluck from the memory a rooted sorrow,
Raze out the written troubles of the brain,
And with some sweet oblivious antidote
Cleanse the stuffed bosom of that perilous stuff
Which weighs upon the heart?

—William Shakespeare,
Macbeth

Ms. A, a 39-year-old, never married, white Protestant executive secretary, seeks consultation for "feeling terrible all my life." As long as she can recall, she has felt shy, inadequate, guilty, and bad. She has chronic sleep difficulties and feels tired much of the time.

A hard worker, she has found work comforting because of the structure the rules of the workplace provide and because she feels her productivity to some degree justifies her otherwise unworthy existence. Lack of energy, easy fatigability, anxious distractibility, and difficulty in concentrating all interfere with her efficiency at the office, but she works extra hours to overcompensate. She has not asked for a raise in years. Regarded as an ideal, loyal, if slightly sad and remote employee, she maintains only superficial relationships with her co-workers. Some take advantage of her good nature, having discovered that she never gets angry. Long work hours have relieved her of the discomfort of lonely nights at home, but the demands of her job and her unexpressed tension with her co-workers have lately worsened her depres-

3

sion. This is what has led her to seek treatment.

Ms. A has tried dating but feels that she is in "a glass box": she dares not let people get too close to her lest they see how contemptible she really is. Although a reasonably attractive woman, she feels unlovable, dressing frumpily, with clumsily applied makeup. Her relationships have been brief and unsatisfying. She generally has sought to gratify her boyfriends' wishes without asserting her own, never getting angry until after the relationship has ended. Afterward, she fatalistically sees the outcome as proof of her unlovability.

In several years of twice weekly psychodynamic psychotherapy, Ms. A had explored her painful childhood, characterized by a controlling, distant, narcissistic mother and a more approving but almost equally distant father. The eldest of four children, she was given early responsibility for the care of her siblings and lost the opportunity for much of her own childhood. Psychotherapy gave her insight into her melancholy character but did not alleviate her depressed symptoms. The focus was principally on the past. Dr. Brown, her psychiatrist, albeit generally kindly, interpreted her childhood and her despondent dreams but offered neither a diagnosis nor a direction for her future. Ms. A felt the doctor implied that she must *want* to feel the way she did, an idea that had indeed guiltily crossed her own mind at times. She also felt that Dr. Brown gradually came to share her discouragement. Never able to address her ambivalent feelings about the therapy, she eventually dropped out. Several briefer episodes of psychotherapy had followed a similar pattern.

Ms. A cannot not recall a period of longer than 6 days when she felt really happy. Most happy events bring only transient pleasure, which then fades back into the usual gloom. She reported two possible episodes of major depression following a breakup with a boyfriend and a job reversal. On both occasions she sought psychotherapy, once with Dr. Brown and once with a social worker. She had been given diazepam for a brief period after one of these crises but had never been offered antidepressant medication. There was no history of mania or substance abuse. She often felt life was not worth living but had never made suicidal plans or attempts.

Ms. A's presentation is typical for a dysthymic patient. Not only does Ms. A meet the DSM-IV symptomatic and temporal criteria for dysthymic disorder (see Table 1–1), she is also female, single, and passive. She has been depressed for essentially as long as she can recall. Her previous psychiatric treatment has consisted entirely of psychotherapy, and this has focused exclusively on her past, reinforcing her own sense that she has a characterological flaw and will always remain this way.

Table 1–1. DSM-IV diagnostic criteria for dysthymic disorder (300.4)

A. Depressed mood for most of the day, for more days than not, as indicated either by subjective account or observation by others, for at least two years. **Note:** In children and adolescents, mood can be irritable and duration must be at least 1 year.

B. Presence while depressed, of two (or more) of the following:

    (1) poor appetite or overeating
    (2) insomnia or hypersomnia
    (3) low energy or fatigue
    (4) low self-esteem
    (5) poor concentration or difficulty making decisions
    (6) feelings of hopelessness

C. During the 2-year period (1 year for children or adolescents) of the disturbance, the person has never been without the symptoms in Criteria A and B for more than 2 months at a time.

D. No Major Depressive Episode has been present during the first 2 years of the disturbance (1 year for children and adolescents); i.e., the disturbance is not better accounted for by chronic Major Depressive Disorder, or Major Depressive Disorder, In Partial Remission.

    Note: There may have been a previous Major Depressive Episode provided there was a full remission (no significant signs or symptoms for 2 months) before development of the Dysthymic Disorder. In addition, after the initial 2 years (1 year in children and adolescents) of Dysthymic Disorder, there may be superimposed episodes of Major Depressive Disorder, in which case both diagnoses may be given when the criteria are met for a Major Depressive Episode.

E. There has never been a Manic Episode, a Mixed Episode, or a Hypomanic Episode, and criteria have never been met for Cyclothymic Disorder.

F. The disturbance does not occur exclusively during the course of a chronic Psychotic Disorder, such as Schizophrenia or Delusional Disorder.

G. The symptoms are not due to the direct physiological effects of a substance (e.g., a drug of abuse, a medication) or a general medical condition (e.g., hypothyroidism).

H. The symptoms cause clinically significant distress or impairment in social, occupational, or other important areas of functioning.

Specify if:
    Early Onset: if onset is before age 21 years
    Late Onset: if onset is age 21 years or older

Source. Reprinted with permission from American Psychiatric Association: *Diagnostic and Statistical Manual of Mental Disorders*, 4th Edition. Washington, DC, American Psychiatric Association, 1994, p. 349. Copyright 1994 by American Psychiatric Association.

Should the Therapist Feel Hopeless Because the Patient Does?

Many psychotherapists probably do become demoralized when faced with a dysthymic patient. When a patient presents with lifelong depression, the despair is often contagious. The therapist's initial sympathy may give way to boredom or irritation, or the therapist may betray his or her sense of the patient's overwhelming problems in setting low expectations and indefinite goals for treatment. Because they are depressed, dysthymic patients generally expect to fail and expect people to give up on them. It is easy to collude unwittingly with such despair. If that happens, the psychotherapy is doomed.

But no, the therapist should not be discouraged just because the dysthymic patient is. The pervasive hopelessness is simply a symptom of depression—*the* symptom, perhaps; the late Gerald L. Klerman, M.D., used to characterize depression as a disease of hopelessness and helplessness. To give in to that hopelessness is to concede the battle at the outset. Rather, it is important that the therapist meet that chronic pessimism with equal and opposite therapeutic optimism.

In fact there is good reason for hope. Antidepressant medication, psychotherapy, and their combination all may be effective treatments for dysthymic disorder. When a patient like Ms. A improves, it is extremely gratifying not only for her but also for her therapist. This book addresses several approaches to chronic depression: medication, psychotherapy, and the particular psychotherapeutic approach of interpersonal psychotherapy (IPT). In contrast to the treatment Ms. A had received, IPT is a forward-looking, optimistic, time-limited, and active therapy. IPT has demonstrated benefits in the treatment of various forms of depression and other psychiatric disorders. There is preliminary evidence that it helps patients with dysthymic disorder as well.

What Should the Therapist Do?

In evaluating a case like Ms. A's, the mental health professional should consider the full range of available treatments. General medical conditions that "mimic" depression (e.g., hypothyroidism, antihypertensive medications) must be ruled out. The best proven and fastest treatment for dysthymic disorder is antidepressant pharmacotherapy (Markowitz 1994), which Ms. A has never even tried, and which surely deserves consideration. Medication might produce a full or partial remission of symptoms. Dysthymic patients respond to standard doses of antidepressant medications (i.e., the disorder can be treated in the same manner as major depression).

Psychotherapy Adjunctive to Medication

It is possible that Ms. A has had enough of psychotherapy for a while and might find pharmacotherapy alone sufficient treatment. More likely, however, a depression-focused psychotherapy like IPT or cognitive-behavior therapy (CBT) (Beck et al. 1979) might help her to deal with residual depressive symptoms. Perhaps equally important, many patients who respond dramatically to antidepressant medications (Kramer 1993) find themselves happy—often for the first time in their lives—and yet bewildered about how to behave under these strange new circumstances (Markowitz 1993). Psychotherapy can help such patients to rethink who they are and what their goals can and should be in their newfound state of euthymia.

Psychotherapy Alone

Let us suppose that Ms. A refused antidepressant medication or that she tried medication and, after numerous trials of adequate dosage and duration, proved to have "treatment-resistant" (Roose and Glassman 1990) dysthymic disorder. Psychotherapy would represent the crucial remaining treatment alternative. The question then would arise: which psychotherapy to use? As I shall discuss at length, not all psychotherapies appear equal in the treatment of mood disorders (see Chapter 2).

Time-limited, focused therapies like IPT and CBT, designed to treat a syndrome rather than to overhaul character, have been demonstrated to work in randomized controlled clinical trials. Other individual psychotherapies may or may not be effective, but most have not been tested; hence their practitioners must depend on belief rather than data to bolster their claims of efficacy. I believe that the time has passed when practitioners could apply a single treatment to all comers on a "Procrustean couch." Just as pharmacotherapists do not give the same medication to all patients, psychotherapists must learn varied approaches for varied conditions or at least know when to refer patients to therapists who know such approaches. And psychotherapists must learn to use the available, admittedly still fragmentary, research evidence to decide when to prescribe one treatment rather than another. In the case of dysthymic disorder the evidence on efficacy is limited, but arguments can be made on behalf of both IPT and CBT.

Facts About Dysthymic Disorder

Dysthymic Disorder Is Prevalent, Expensive, Morbid, and Comorbid

Definitions

In its short history, chronic depression has provoked considerable controversy. Until 1980 most chronically depressed patients were considered to have a character disorder: "depressive neurosis," a depressive or masochistic personality. Based on this psychoanalytically derived definition, the treatment of choice was considered long-term psychodynamic psychotherapy, although even that often was believed to have a poor prognosis (Markowitz 1994).

Dysthymic disorder.   In 1980, DSM-III (American Psychiatric Association 1980) changed all that. Responding to the seminal work of Hagop Akiskal, M.D., and others (Akiskal 1983; Akiskal et al. 1980, 1981), which suggested that chronic depression was a mood disorder that often responded to antidepressant medication, the authors of DSM-III reclassified dysthymic disorder as an affective (mood) disorder rather than a character disorder. This was among the most radical, and ultimately most useful, nosological shifts in DSM-III (Kocsis and Frances 1987).

The concept of dysthymic disorder has been preserved in DSM-III-R (American Psychiatric Association 1987), which changed the name of the disorder to dysthymia, changed the symptom criteria somewhat, and added distinctions for early (before age 21) and late (21 and older) onset and for primary and secondary subtypes. Because dysthymic disorder is associated with high comorbidity, many clinicians considered it a form of secondary demoralization in the wake of other psychiatric or medical disorders. Yet research indicates that most dysthymic episodes are primary, *preceding* the onset of other disorders (Kovacs et al. 1984; Markowitz et al. 1992a). DSM-III-R also differentiates dysthymia, which has an insidious onset, from major depressive episode, chronic type, in which patients develop sufficient symptomatology to meet criteria for a major depressive episode within 2 years of onset. It is as yet unclear whether these distinctions have clinical significance; for example, preliminary data from a multicenter pharmaceutical trial comparing sertraline and imipramine have found essentially equal responses to both medications in patients with double depression and chronic major depression (M. B. Keller et al., unpublished observations, 1995).

The advent of DSM-IV (American Psychiatric Association 1994) brought a new definitional dilemma. Researchers familiar with dysthymic disorder, as the 1994 version again titles it, felt that the neurovegetative emphasis of the DSM-III-R symptom criteria did not adequately reflect the more cognitive symptoms with which dysthymic patients characteristically present. Field trials in preparation for DSM-IV empirically evaluated dysthymic patients. They found that the most prevalent symptoms among dysthymic patients in fact tended to be cognitive (e.g., pessimism and low self-esteem) rather than the neurovegetative disturbances (such as sleep or appetite disturbance) prominent in major depression (Keller et al. 1995) (see Table 1–2). Accordingly, researchers proposed a set of symptom criteria for dysthymic disorder reflecting this cognitive emphasis. In a somewhat political compromise, DSM-IV retained the DSM-III-R criteria for purposes of continuity (see Table 1–1), relegating the research criteria to an appendix (see Table 1–3). In practice, the two definitions appear to encompass the same patient population.

Double depression. Another diagnostic controversy surrounding dysthymic disorder is its overlap with major depressive disorder. Symptom criteria for the two disorders are similar, differing mainly in the number of symptoms needed. It is almost inevitable that, at some point in the long course of his or her depressive illness, the dysthymic individual will become stressed by some untoward event and develop two additional depressive symptoms for at least 2 weeks. At this point the patient will also meet criteria for major depression, or *double depression* (major depression superimposed on dysthymic disorder) (Keller and Shapiro 1982). The DSM-IV Field Trial on Mood Disorders found that 79% of 191 subjects meeting diagnostic criteria for DSM-III-R dysthymia also had a lifetime history of major depression (Keller et al. 1995).

Our experience at Cornell University Medical College has made us skeptical about the concept of double depression (Keller and Shapiro 1982; Keller et al. 1983). We doubt that this represents the concurrence of two qualitatively distinct mood disorders; rather, we conceptualize double depression as evidence of symptomatic fluctuation or exacerbation of a single, chronic depressive disorder. Although "doubly depressed" patients may suffer still more symptoms—greater acute severity—than those who meet criteria for dysthymic disorder alone, response to treatment does not appear to differ (Marin et al. 1994). On the other hand, less symptomatic patients with "pure" dysthymic disorder may have a higher rate of placebo response than double depressives (see Chapter 2). For clinical purposes it generally seems reasonable to consider pure dysthymic disorder and double depression indistinguishable beyond symptom severity.

Table 1–2. Symptom prevalence of dysthymic subjects in the DSM-IV mood disorder field trials

Rank	Symptom	Frequency (%)
1	Low self-esteem	84
2	Pessimism	77
3	Feelings of inadequacy	73
4	Social withdrawal	71
5	Loss of interest or pleasure	70
6	Low energy or fatigue	66
7	Hopelessness	65
8	Irritability or excessive anger	65
9	Brooding	65
10	Decreased effectiveness or productivity	62
11	Poor concentration	60
12	Self-pity	59
13	Difficulty making decisions	59
14	Less talkative	58
15	Tearfulness or crying	54
16	Insomnia	50
17	Feeling slowed down	50
18	Inability to respond to praise or rewards	47
19	Overeating	44
20	Recurrent thoughts of death or suicide	43
21	Restlessness	41
22	Hypersomnia	38
23	Poor appetite	32

Source. Based on interviews of 193 subjects; reprinted with permission from Keller MB, Klein DN, Hirschfeld RMA, et al.: "Results of the DSM-IV mood disorders field trial." *American Journal of Psychiatry* 152:843–849, 1995. Copyright 1995 by American Psychiatric Association.

Depressive personality disorder. Another area of clinical controversy concerns *depressive personality.* Within 10 years of the DSM-III reconceptualization of chronic depression as a mood disorder, several articles were published resurrecting the historical "depressive personality" (Schneider 1958) as a potential personality disorder (Hirschfeld and Holzer 1994; Klein 1990; Klein and Miller 1993; Phillips et al. 1990). One result of this flurry of interest is that DSM-IV lists depressive

Table 1–3. Research/appendix DSM-IV diagnostic criteria

"Alternative research criterion B for dysthymic disorder"

B. Presence, while depressed, of three (or more) of the following:

1. Low self-esteem or self-confidence, or feelings of inadequacy
2. Feelings of pessimism, despair, or hopelessness
3. Generalized loss of interest or pleasure
4. Social withdrawal
5. Chronic fatigue or tiredness
6. Feelings of guilt, brooding about the past
7. Subjective feelings of irritability or excessive anger
8. Decreased activity, effectiveness, or productivity
9. Difficulty in thinking, reflected by poor concentration, poor memory, or indecisiveness

Source. Reprinted with permission from American Psychiatric Association: *Diagnostic and Statistical Manual of Mental Disorders*, 4th Edition. Washington, DC, American Psychiatric Association, 1994, p. 718. Copyright 1994 by American Psychiatric Association.

personality disorder in its appendix. Symptoms of depressive personality disorder overlap with dysthymic disorder. They include dejection, gloominess, and unhappiness; a sense of inadequacy, worthlessness, and low self-esteem; self-criticism and blame; brooding and worry; and negativism, pessimism, guilt, and remorse. The text also states that the above symptoms must not "occur exclusively during major depressive episodes" (American Psychiatric Association 1994, p. 732).

We remain unconvinced that depressive personality disorder is either clinically useful or clinically distinguishable from dysthymic disorder. Moreover, we are concerned that it raises the danger of perpetuating a problem that has long plagued dysthymic patients and their treatment: namely, that therapists will treat them for an underlying personality disorder *when their problem is in fact a chronic mood disorder.* A chronic disorder, particularly a lifelong one, can become part of a patient's self-perception. As dysthymic disorder frequently is lifelong, the exclusionary DSM-IV caveat really ought to state that "the above symptoms must not occur during an episode of dysthymic disorder." Because of the difficulty in distinguishing chronic "state" from "trait" in the presence of chronic mood disorder, the clinician should avoid prejudging patients as "character disordered" until the depression has lifted (Bronisch and Klerman 1991; Loranger et al. 1991). Only if dysthymic disorder has failed to respond to specific antidepressant pharmacologic and psychotherapeutic treatments should the therapist entertain the idea of depressive personality disorder. In our experience, such occasions are few indeed.

Prevalence

Dysthymic disorder affects 3% of American adults, which makes it a significant public health problem (Kessler et al. 1994; Weissman et al. 1988). Because dysthymic individuals are likely to seek medical and mental health care (Weissman et al. 1988), the prevalence of dysthymic disorder among psychiatric and other mental health practices is probably much higher. In psychiatric clinics the prevalence ranges as high as 36% (Markowitz et al. 1992a). We have little knowledge of the actual nature of most psychiatric practices, but it is commonly assumed that dysthymic patients account for a substantial proportion of caseloads. Their chronicity assures that if they do not receive effective treatment, they will need ongoing treatment.

DSM-IV implicitly minimizes the severity of dysthymic disorder, according "major" depression its title based on the severity of acute symptoms. Dysthymic disorder, in contrast, has sometimes been called "subsyndromal" and in any case appears "minor" by comparison. This bias seems hardly fair to dysthymic patients, who may carry a lesser short-term burden of symptoms but must live with them for decades unless they find appropriate treatment.

Morbidity

The worst outcome of a mood disorder is suicide. Yet even when depression does not lead patients to kill themselves it causes terrible suffering. Not surprisingly, patients with chronic depression may suffer most. Research has shown that dysthymic patients have more disturbed life courses than those with major depression: more difficulty with relationships, and poorer general health, social functioning, and work functioning (Wells et al. 1992). Thus the disability of the syndrome goes beyond simple symptoms. Dysthymic disorder strips people of basic assets such as confidence, self-assertion, and other interpersonal skills.

Epidemiology of Dysthymic Disorder

Several large national surveys have revealed that chronic depression affects 3% of the U.S. adult population, including 4% of women (Kessler et al. 1994; Weissman et al. 1988). Major depression, although a more obvious condition because of its acute severity, has itself been undertreated (Keller et al. 1992). Because dysthymic disorder can be less obvious—often more or less successfully concealed by the patient and not recognized by practitioners—it may be even more likely to go untreated or undertreated (Weissman and Klerman 1977). Thus dysthymic disorder has a "low profile": patients are with great effort able to "pass" at work and are unlikely to sbe hospitalized unless they develop an exacerbation of symptoms (i.e., double depression).

The Epidemiologic Catchment Area (ECA) study (Weissman et al. 1988), a carefully sampled survey, interviewed more than 18,000 subjects at five sites across the United States between 1980 and 1983. The first large-scale epidemiologic survey of psychiatric disorders, the ECA study identified particular segments of the population at greater risk for having dysthymic disorder. Depending on the site, women were one-and-a-half to three times more likely than men to carry the diagnosis. Adults between the ages of 18 and 64 were at greater risk than those 65 and older. Moreover, researchers found a sex-by-age interaction: lifetime diagnosis of dysthymic disorder was greatest among women between the ages of 45 and 64. Those individuals in the 18- to 44-year-old age range who reported low income—less than $20,000 annually—were also at increased risk (see Table 1–4). Race, education, and employment status did not affect the likelihood of having the diagnosis.

The ECA study also found that dysthymic patients made frequent use of treatment. They were nearly twice as likely as nondysthymic interviewees to report use of general medical care in the past 6 months and more than three times as likely to have sought mental health treatment. Unfortunately, this did not mean that they necessarily received *appropriate* treatment. At the New Haven, Connecticut, site, where psychotropic medications were recorded, dysthymic patients reported an increased use of minor tranquilizers and sedatives as well as antidepressants and lithium relative to nondysthymic subjects. (One wonders whether the antidepressants were given in adequate dosage.)

The National Comorbidity Study (Kessler et al. 1994), another impressive

---

Table 1–4. Features associated with dysthymic disorder

Epidemiologic findings associated with increased prevalence:

    Sex: Women > men

    Age: 18–64 > 65+

    Unmarried if age under 65

    Low income (< $20,000) if age 18–44

Other associated features:

    High comorbidity of other psychiatric disorders

    High usage of health and mental health treatment services

Source. Adapted from Weissman et al. 1988.

large-scale epidemiologic effort using a somewhat different methodology than the ECA study, found a similar high prevalence of dysthymic disorder.

Comorbidity of Dysthymic Disorder

The ECA and National Comorbidity studies, like others of community and clinical samples, found that dysthymic patients rarely carried the diagnosis of dysthymic disorder alone; rather, these patients frequently met criteria for several diagnoses. Dysthymia overlapped frequently with major depression, anxiety disorders, substance abuse, and cluster B and C axis II personality disorders. Dysthymic disorder can also be comorbid with medical disorders and other psychiatric conditions.

Comorbidity may account for clinicians missing or mistreating the diagnosis of dysthymic disorder (Kocsis et al. 1990). It was, again, long thought that dysthymic symptoms might represent demoralization secondary to comorbidity, whereas the opposite seems to be true; in most cases, dysthymic disorder appears first and is then compounded by other mood and anxiety diagnoses (Kovacs et al. 1984). Some of this "comorbidity" may indeed be artifactual; symptoms of dysthymic disorder may overlap with—really, trespass on—other sets of diagnostic criteria such as avoidant personality disorder. If one treats the dysthymic disorder, comorbid conditions frequently melt away (Markowitz 1993). The dysthymia research team at Cornell found that having a comorbid anxiety disorder did not affect the response of dysthymic patients to antidepressant medication (D. Lewinter et al., unpublished observations, 1992).

Tables 1–5 and 1–6 show the frequency of comorbid diagnoses among dysthymic outpatients compared with nondysthymic outpatients in a study at the Payne Whitney Clinic of the New York Hospital (Markowitz et al. 1992a). Research interviews using the Structured Clinical Interview for DSM-III Patient Version (SCID-P) (Spitzer and Williams 1985) and for Personality Disorders (SCID-II) (Spitzer et al. 1986) found dysthymic subjects were more likely to meet criteria for major depression, social phobia, and avoidant, self-defeating, dependent, and borderline personality disorders. Dysthymic disorder was usually of early onset, predating comorbid disorders, and often had not received adequate antidepressant treatment.

Social Morbidity

The chronic low mood and self-doubt that are hallmarks of dysthymic disorder probably account for a second characteristic feature: social and vocational dysfunction (Friedman 1993). Dysthymic patients lead lives of quiet desperation. By expending all of their limited energy, they can strive, often with some success, to look

Table 1–5. Axis I diagnoses: lifetime by Structured Clinical Interview for DSM-III Patient Version (SCID-P)

	Dysthymia (N = 34)		Other (N = 56)	
	n	%	*n*	%
Dysthymic disorder	34	100	0	0
Major depression	23	68	21	38
Bipolar disorder	0	0	6	11
Cyclothymic	1	3	4	7
Schizoaffective disorder	0	0	2	4
Adjustment disorder	1	3	3	5
Obsessive-compulsive disorder	4	12	3	5
Hypochondriasis	1	3	0	0
Somatization disorder	1	3	2	4
Bulimia	4	12	2	4
Panic disorder	9	26	11	20
Agoraphobia	1	3	2	4
Simple phobia	4	12	2	4
Social phobia	5	15	1	2
Posttraumatic stress disorder	4	12	5	9
Generalized anxiety disorder	4	12	5	9
Substance abuse	8	24	12	21
Schizophrenia	0	0	5	9
Dementia	0	0	1	2
Organic mood disorder	0	0	5	9
Other	2	6	2	4
None[a]	0	0	3	5
Mean number of axis I diagnoses/ subject (excluding dysthymic disorder)	**2.1**		**1.7**	

[a]By definition, all dysthymic subjects met criteria for one axis I disorder. Two (6%) dysthymic subjects did not meet criteria for a comorbid axis I disorder.

Source. Reprinted with permission from Markowitz JC, Moran ME, Kocsis JH, et al.: "Prevalence and Comorbidity of Dysthymic Disorder Among Psychiatric Outpatients." *Journal of Affective Disorders* 24:63–71, 1992a.

Table 1–6.   Axis II diagnoses by Structured Clinical Interview for
DSM-III—Personality Disorders (SCID-II)

	Dysthymia (N = 34)		Other (N = 55)	
	n	%	*n*	%
Cluster A				
Paranoid	1	3	6	11
Schizoid	0	0	0	0
Schizotypal	4	12	2	4
Cluster B				
Borderline	8	24	3	6
Histrionic	4	12	11	20
Narcissistic	2	6	6	11
Antisocial	0	0	1	2
Cluster C				
Avoidant	11	32	1	2
Dependent	7	21	3	5
Obsessive compulsive	2	6	6	11
Passive aggressive	0	0	2	4
Not otherwise specified	6	18	14	26
Self-defeating	12	35	1	2
No axis II diagnosis	5	15	15	27
Mean number of axis II diagnoses/subject	**1.7**		**1.0**	

Source.   Reprinted with permission from Markowitz JC, Moran ME, Kocsis JH, et al.: "Prevalence and Comorbidity of Dysthymic Disorder Among Psychiatric Outpatients." *Journal of Affective Disorders* 24:63–71, 1992a.

outwardly "normal" at work. Indeed, dysthymic individuals tend to be hard and loyal workers, struggling to justify their self-perceived lack of worth through labor. Such guilt may drive them to compensate for low energy, poor concentration, and a sense of being overwhelmed by their environment.

Socially, however, dysthymic patients have more difficulty. Work provides known rules to follow, whereas social intercourse is more complex and treacherous. (One dysthymic woman, of considerable work accomplishments, said, "I've spoken to the CEOs of corporations without such difficulty. It's when I have to talk to another parent at a bus stop that I'm completely lost.") Dysthymic patients often have limited social experience because of the early onset of their illness; they often report lifelong shyness and social avoidance, if not social phobia. And whereas at work they can masquerade in normalcy, dysthymic individuals may often see relationships as hopeless; getting close to another person can reveal only the inner "badness" they themselves feel, and will inevitably lead to rejection. Dysthymic individuals characteristically have difficulty with the social issues depression inhibits: self-assertion, expression of appropriate anger, and social risk taking.

One attractive woman described dating as "out of the question" because of the way she felt; she knew she would have to be rejected. She described her social life as "living in a Lucite box"; the goal was not to allow anyone to get close enough to see how messed up she really was.

Another woman, whose life from earliest childhood had been a series of betrayals and abandonments, passively acceded to painful social situations rather than expressing objections or anger. She justified this behavior by saying that she did not want to "make waves"; the annoyances people caused were not worth commenting on, and who was she to object?

These social difficulties have been documented with the Social Adjustment Scale (Cassano et al. 1990; Kocsis et al. 1988a; Stewart et al. 1988; Weissman and Bothwell 1976) and the Inventory for Interpersonal Problems (Horowitz et al. 1988). These studies have also shown that dysthymic patients have difficulty in enjoying leisure time; they are frequently just miserable. (It may be that work provides a useful structure without which dysthymic patients feel still worse.) Yet dysthymic difficulties in social and vocational functioning (Kocsis et al. 1988b; Stewart et al. 1988) and self-perception of interpersonal competency (Markowitz et al. 1996) improve rapidly (i.e., in 6–10 weeks) in patients who respond to antidepressant medication. The interpersonal difficulties of dysthymic patients provide an important part of the rationale for treating them with IPT. Dysthymic patients indeed often can address their social difficulties in IPT.

Dysthymic Individuals As Patients

Chronically depressed people are not only discouraged themselves, they also discourage those in their environment. Research has shown that although people initially respond to a depressed person with sympathy, that sympathy soon wears thin and is replaced by irritation and withdrawal (Klerman et al. 1984). In therapy, too, dysthymic patients have historically carried a poor prognosis. They often have been described as "discouraging," "self-defeating" patients whose chronicity of illness may unduly daunt therapists. One expert in dysthymic psychotherapy, acknowledging the difficulty in treating these patients, cautiously called them "bears." In fact, dysthymic disorder can often be effectively treated with pharmacotherapy, focused psychotherapy, or a combination of the two. It is crucial, however, that the therapist remain optimistic in the face of chronic symptoms and the patient's own discouragement.

In my experience, dysthymic patients are acutely sensitive to the demoralization of those around them. Therapists who lack confidence will lose potentially treatable dysthymic patients. I often consult on patients who have been in lengthy psychotherapies in which, it seems clear, both patient and therapist have long tacitly agreed that there is little hope. Not only is pragmatic optimism one of the features of IPT, the structured-treatment framework provides support for therapists to fall back on when they might otherwise feel discouraged.

In summary, dysthymic disorder is frequently misunderstood, underdiagnosed, and mistreated. It is in fact a medical illness that is prevalent, morbid, and treatable.

CHAPTER 2
Treatment of Dysthymic Disorder

So weary with disasters, tugged with fortune,
That I would set my life on any chance,
To mend it or be rid on't.

—William Shakespeare,
Macbeth

The Rise of Psychopharmacology

The reclassification of dysthymic disorder as a mood disorder in DSM-III (American Psychiatric Association 1980) encouraged the use of antidepressant medication in treatment. Key figures in this development are Hagop Akiskal, M.D., who reported the success of antidepressant pharmacotherapy in open clinical trials (Akiskal 1983), and James Kocsis, M.D., who conducted the first controlled trial to show that imipramine was more effective than placebo in the treatment of dysthymic patients (Kocsis et al. 1988a). Kocsis and colleagues also showed that chronic difficulties in social and vocational functioning could improve significantly within 6 weeks of beginning antidepressant pharmacotherapy (Kocsis et al. 1988b).

Pharmacotherapy of chronic and lifelong depressive syndromes has since generated great interest. A variety of studies have demonstrated the acute benefits of antidepressant medication for chronically depressed patients (Bakish et al. 1993; Bersani et al. 1991; Harrison et al. 1986; Hellerstein et al. 1993; Versiani 1994; for a review, see Howland 1991). Tricyclic antidepressants (Kocsis et al. 1988a, 1994;

Stewart et al. 1988; Thase et al. 1996; Versiani 1994), selective serotonin reuptake inhibitors (SSRIs) (Guelfi and Wiseman 1995; Hellerstein et al. 1993; Kocsis et al. 1994; Thase et al. 1996), serotonin-2 receptor antagonists (Bakish et al. 1993; Bersani et al. 1991), and monoamine oxidase inhibitors (Harrison et al. 1986; Versiani 1994) have demonstrated efficacy in the short-term treatment of subjects with double depression, pure dysthymic disorder, or both. Medication can suppress symptoms and improve functioning. Moreover, recent controlled studies support clinical experience (Kocsis et al. 1991) in demonstrating that ongoing pharmacotherapy prevents relapse and recurrence of chronic depression (Kocsis et al. 1996). Unfortunately, few factors have been found that predict whether a patient will respond to medication (Kocsis et al. 1989).

Kocsis and colleagues (1996) treated dysthymic patients with desipramine alone at dosages of up to 300 mg daily. The mean dosage was over 200 mg/day. After patients had been stabilized for 6 months on desipramine, they were randomly assigned either to continue desipramine or to be gradually tapered to placebo over a month; patients were then followed with monthly assessments for 2 years. Results demonstrated that patients who remained on desipramine for the entire 2½ years had a very small chance of relapsing into dysthymic disorder. In contrast, more than one-half of the patients who were randomized to placebo relapsed during the follow-up period. This study indicates that maintenance antidepressant medication can have ongoing benefits for dysthymic patients but that stopping medication, at least after 6 months, carries the risk of relapse.

On the basis of available evidence, antidepressant medication should be considered the treatment of choice for dysthymic patients. Research evidence for the efficacy of psychotherapy in dysthymic disorder is far less solid. From the outcome literature just reviewed and from years of clinical experience in working with dysthymic patients, I distill the following points:

1. *Many dysthymic patients clearly do have mood disorders.*   If these patients truly had "depressive personality disorder," we would not expect them to respond acutely to antidepressant medications.

2. *At least one-half of dysthymic patients respond, often dramatically, to antidepressant medication.*   Despite once having been thought to have a poor prognosis (Akiskal et al. 1980), chronic mood states often remit with antidepressant pharmacotherapy. In general, antidepressant response rates have been similar across medications and depressive subtypes. Although we cannot accurately predict which patients will and will not respond to antidepressant medication—I have been fooled

many times, in both directions—many dysthymic patients clearly deserve a robust antidepressant medication trial. The history I most fear, and hear, when evaluating dysthymic patients is that they have had years of unfocused psychotherapy that have yielded insight but no symptomatic improvement, apparently without the therapist ever having entertained the thought of a pharmacotherapy trial.

3. Not only symptoms improve, but also social and vocational functioning.   As noted in Chapter 1, dysthymic patients who respond to medication improve across the board. One dysthymic researcher has joked that a benefit of practicing pharmacotherapy with dysthymic patients is that "after a while, you get wedding invitations." It is true: medication alone can help improve social competence for many patients.

4. Medication treats a chronic depressive illness "state," not a personality "trait." This is what I call the "Peter Kramer–*Listening to Prozac*" phenomenon. The late 1980s and the early 1990s saw the growth in popularity of SSRIs: antidepressant medications such as fluoxetine (Prozac), sertraline (Zoloft), paroxetine (Paxil), and fluvoxamine (Luvox). These medications are not evidently more effective than older antidepressant medications, such as tricyclic antidepressants and monoamine oxidase inhibitors. But because they do have fewer side effects, by and large, many patients find them more tolerable than tricyclics. SSRIs are also less dangerous when taken in overdose, and—perhaps most important—the simplicity of their dosing schedule has encouraged their use by nonpsychiatric physicians who were uncomfortable prescribing the older medications. With the popularity of these medications—fluoxetine, as the first, received wide media attention as a "wonder drug"—came the idea of "cosmetic psychopharmacology."

The concept of cosmetic pharmacology, spread in the media by Peter Kramer's *Listening to Prozac* (1993), suggests that medications like fluoxetine can not only relieve mood disorders but change underlying personality. This in turn revives an old issue in the "state" versus "trait" phenomenon. Personality is presumed to be a lifelong and stable trait. Yet clinicians have long observed that patients in the midst of an acute crisis or episode of illness may not behave in characteristic ways; that is, the state of acute illness confounds the trait. Hence clinicians have learned not to diagnose axis II personality disorders in the presence of an acute episode of major depression, mania, and so forth. Only when the state has been treated can underlying personality traits be safely adjudged.

This state-versus-trait issue is crucial to the treatment of dysthymic disorder. Dysthymic disorder is a quintessential example of a *chronic state:* an episode of illness so long-standing and apparently stable that the therapist and especially the patient both may consider it to be the bedrock of personality. A central argument of this book is that *personality should not be prejudged in dysthymic patients.* As noted in Chapter 1, dysthymic patients often consider themselves to have depressive personalities and often meet criteria for depressively tinged comorbid axis II diagnoses such as avoidant, dependent, self-defeating, and borderline personality disorder. Yet treatment of dysthymic disorder may reveal this apparent trait to have been a lengthy state.

Hence the so-called cosmetic pharmacology of medications like fluoxetine in all likelihood represents the stripping away of underlying dysthymic symptoms, leaving the patient euthymic. This is not cosmetic and is not a change in personality trait but rather the relief of a chronic mood state.

Psychotherapy of Dysthymic Disorder[1]

Before 1980, when DSM-III defined dysthymic disorder, chronically depressed patients were considered to have depressive temperaments, depressive neuroses, or depressive characters. The treatment of choice was accordingly long-term psychodynamic psychotherapy or psychoanalysis. Unfortunately, no research was done to test the efficacy of this treatment.

The first research discussion of psychotherapy of dysthymic disorder dates back to 1984, when chronic depression had recently been reclassified as a mood disorder and researchers were exploring benefits of antidepressant medication for its treatment. Weissman and Akiskal (1984) then made a modest proposal for psychotherapeutic approaches to dysthymic disorder. Noting that only "indirect" evidence existed for psychotherapeutic efficacy in chronic depression, they proposed assessing the efficacy of short-term therapies—interpersonal, cognitive, or behavioral—either alone or in combination with medication.

How far have we come? In the intervening years, diagnosis has been honed with greater precision in DSM-III-R and DSM-IV (American Psychiatric Association 1987, 1994). We better understand the prevalence, morbidity, and comorbidity of dysthymic disorder. Dysthymic disorder clearly represents a public health problem.

---

[1] The remainder of this chapter is adapted from Markowitz JC: "Psychotherapy of Dysthymic Disorder." *American Journal of Psychiatry* 151:1114–1121, 1994.

Controlled clinical trials have also shown the efficacy of time-limited manualized psychotherapies for acute major depression (Beck et al. 1979; Elkin et al. 1989; Klerman et al. 1984) and for other axis I disorders (Klerman and Weissman 1993) but not for dysthymic disorder. Compared with other areas of dysthymia research, psychotherapy has received little attention. Yet dysthymic patients are known to make frequent use of mental health services (Weissman et al. 1988), and it is commonly assumed that they comprise substantial proportions of many if not most psychotherapeutic practices.

The rationale for antidysthymic psychotherapy should be clear (see Table 2–1). Roughly one-half of dysthymic patients do not respond to antidepressant medication. Others develop intolerable side effects, hypomania (Akiskal 1981), or are simply too fearful to take pills. Pregnancy and other medical conditions may be contraindications to medication. Patients who experience only a partial response to pharmacotherapy may need adjunctive psychotherapy.

Antidepressant psychotherapies have been shown to treat acute mood disorders and may benefit dysthymic patients as well. Psychotherapies presumably work by a different mechanism and therefore may yield different benefits than pharmacotherapy. Whereas medication works faster and most rapidly alleviates physical symptoms of depression, psychotherapies (and interpersonal psychotherapy [IPT] in particular) may help depressed patients develop social skills (DiMascio et al. 1979; Klerman et al. 1974; Weissman et al. 1981).

Three percent of American adults have dysthymic disorder, dysthymic individuals frequently use mental health services, and many will visit nonpsychiatrists who

---

Table 2–1. Rationale for psychotherapy of dysthymic disorder

Antidepressant psychotherapy versus medication

    Medication nonresponse

    Intolerance of medication side effects

    Medical contraindication to pharmacotherapy

    Patient preference (refusal of medication)

Psychotherapy factors

    Partial medication response (indication for adjunctive psychotherapy)

    Demonstrated efficacy of psychotherapies for acute depressive episodes

    Potential benefits for social skills of dysthymic patients

    Few psychotherapeutic side effects

    Role for nonpsychiatric psychotherapists

cannot prescribe medication. Thus, despite the ascendancy of antidepressant medication as the de facto standard treatment for this condition, antidysthymic psychotherapy should not be prematurely abandoned. The limitations of antidepressant medication, as well as the treatment preference of patients and therapists, argue for the development of effective psychotherapeutic interventions.

To review psychotherapy research on dysthymic disorder, I culled selections under "dysthymia," "dysthymic disorder," "chronic depression," and "psychotherapy" from *Excerpta Medica: Psychiatry* (Database on CD-ROM, SilverPlatter Version 3.11, Amsterdam, Elsevier Science Publishers, 1980–1994). All studies that reported psychotherapy treatment outcome for dysthymic patients were included except studies of late-life chronic major depression. Distinctions to keep in mind for this literature include those between "pure" dysthymic disorder and "double depression" (i.e., major depression superimposed on dysthymic disorder), early- versus late-onset dysthymic disorder, full versus partial remission, and treatment with psychotherapy alone versus combined pharmacopsychotherapy.

Psychotherapy Studies

Akiskal in 1980 cited the psychopharmacologist Donald Klein, M.D., and "[referring] clinicians' beliefs" in claiming that chronic depression not only responded to pharmacotherapy but that "various forms of psychotherapy [were] equally disappointing" (Akiskal et al. 1980, p. 778). Although it is difficult to find explicit statements in the literature, this seems to have been the general view of psychotherapy outcome with long-depressed patients; because of ingrained hopelessness, masochism, and self-sabotage, dysthymic patients tended to do poorly. One relatively recent description of masochistic character, which that author says differs from but often overlaps with dysthymic disorder, captures this spirit of clinical pessimism:

> They are the patients who unconsciously provoke their therapists either to give up on them, or sadistically abuse them with premature and unempathic interpretations, or pejoratively dismiss them with the misdiagnosis of borderline personality disorder or passive aggressive personality disorder. . . . But whatever the unconscious motives may be in an individual case, the final behavioral outcome is the achievement of what Theodor Reik called "victory through defeat," and often the defeat is a failed psychiatric treatment (Simons 1987).

Yet news from the psychotherapy front is not entirely bleak. We surveyed 43 established clinicians and researchers in dysthymic disorder about their experience in treating forms of chronic depression. Thirty-two (74%) responded, including 25 (58%) who completed questionnaires. They reported a mean 70.7% rate of improvement among patients treated either with psychotherapy alone or with combined psychopharmacotherapy (Markowitz et al. 1990). This impressionistic finding contradicted the apparently prevailing view of a grim prognosis.

The few psychotherapy studies of dysthymic disorder generally suffer from methodological weakness, small sample size, or both. Psychotherapeutic efficacy in these studies should be weighed against the low response rate of dysthymic patients to placebos, which ranges from less than 15% for double depression (Kocsis et al. 1988a) to 19%–28% for "pure" dysthymic disorder (Hellerstein et al. 1993; Kocsis et al. 1994; Thase et al. 1996). Methodological issues include the number of psychotherapists involved, the generalizability of their technique, use of adherence monitoring, and characteristics of the patient population (e.g., inclusion of prior treatment failures). Readers should also note the studies' definitions of response and length of follow-up.

Psychodynamic Psychotherapy and Psychoanalysis

Recent psychoanalytic literature is relatively meager on depression generally and dysthymic disorder particularly (Cohen et al. 1954; Jacobson 1971; Simons 1987; Stone 1986). There has been little effort to differentiate acute and chronic forms of depression. The best work (e.g., Arieti and Bemporad 1978; Bemporad 1976) provided rich insights into the minds and feeling states of depressed patients and suggested interpersonal techniques but offered no outcome data. Some authors in the 1970s repeated the historical contention that psychodynamic psychotherapy was the treatment of choice for people with chronic depression (Chodoff 1972; Jacobson 1971). Unfortunately, there has been no published psychodynamic research on dysthymic disorder since 1984 and no treatment manuals or trials. Reviews of supportive dynamic psychotherapy have not addressed dysthymic disorder (Rockland 1989, 1993). Thus, although long-term psychodynamic therapy continues to be frequently prescribed for dysthymic patients, there is no evidence that either short- or long-term psychodynamic treatment benefits such patients. What we as dysthymia treatment researchers hear from an admittedly selected sample of psychodynamic treatment failures is that years of such treatment have often provided insight into depression but little relief from it.

A possible difficulty with a psychoanalytically oriented approach to dysthymic disorder may involve the confusion of chronic mood state with personality trait. In dysthymic disorder of insidious early onset, with chronicity often as long as the patient can recall, personality trait and chronic mood disorder have the greatest opportunity to be confused by both patient and therapist. Using a conflictual rather than a medical model of psychopathology, psychoanalytically oriented therapists may tend to "blame the victim" by assigning the patient responsibility for his or her mood disorder (Cooper 1985). Dysthymic patients are the first to attribute their problems to a personality defect. Analytic abstinence and neutrality may also be counterproductive for patients whose outlooks are so distorted by depressed mood that they may need active support, even therapeutic cheerleading, to balance their perspective.

Cognitive-Behavior Therapy

Cognitive-behavior therapy (CBT) is a structured, time-limited psychotherapy developed by Beck and colleagues (1979). Its efficacy in the treatment of acute major depression has been demonstrated in multiple clinical trials. The focus of CBT is on the "automatic" negative thoughts that depressed patients report about themselves, their situations, and their future. Through rational discussions with their therapists and written and behavioral homework assignments, patients learn to modify irrationally negative thoughts; as they do, depression improves.

Several cognitive approaches have been tested for treating dysthymic patients (see Table 2–2). Gonzalez and colleagues (1985) studied 113 patients treated with 12 individual or group 2-hour sessions of a skills-training oriented psychoeducational approach over 2 months, plus 1- and 6-month follow-up sessions. They found that more subjects with acute major depression by Research Diagnostic Criteria (RDC) (Spitzer et al. 1978) recovered (75%) than did those with (chronic) intermittent depression (43%) or double depression (27%). Recovery was defined as 8 weeks essentially symptom free and a rating of 1 or 2 on the Longitudinal Interval Follow-up Evaluation (R. Shapiro and M. Keller, unpublished manuscript, 1979). Follow-up varied between 1 and 3 years. The number of therapists is not stated.

de Jong et al. (1986) treated 30 unmedicated inpatients meeting DSM-III criteria for both dysthymic disorder and major depression who had family histories negative for mood disorder. A 2- to 3-month trial of combined activity scheduling, social competence training, and cognitive restructuring yielded a higher response rate (60%) than cognitive restructuring alone (30%) or waiting list status (10%). Response was defined as meeting two of three criteria: posttreatment Beck Depression Inventory (BDI) (Beck et al. 1979) ≤ 14 or $\geq 50\%$ reduction from pretreatment BDI, and $\geq 50\%$ reduction from pretreatment on two infrequently used treatment scales.

Table 2–2. Reports of cognitive-behavior therapy of dysthymic disorder

Study	N	Intensity	Response (%)	Follow-up	Remarks
Gonzalez et al. 1985	28 dys 26 double	12 2-hour sessions/ 8 weeks	43 27	12–36	IP or GP RDC criteria
de Jong et al. 1986	10 double	2- to 3-month inpatient	60[a]	6	DSM-III criteria CR and waiting list comparisons
Fennell and Teasdale 1982	5	20 sessions/ 12 weeks	20	—	RDC criteria Ham-D 23 → 17
Harpin et al. 1982	6	20 sessions/ 10 weeks + 25 mg TCA	33	6	Ham-D 26 → 16 waiting list control
Stravynski et al. 1991	6	15 sessions	67	6	DSM-III criteria Ham-D 24 ≥ 9
McCullough 1991	20	14–44 C-BASP sessions	50	24	DSM-III criteria 9 remitted at 2 years
Mercier et al. 1992	8 dys 7 double	12–16 sessions	38 43	6	DSM-III criteria
Thase et al. 1994	15 double 7 chronic major	16 sessions	27 29		
Totals	**138**		**39**		

[a]1–2 early dropout(s) omitted from outcome analysis.

Note. Dys = dysthymic; double = double depression; IP = individual psychotherapy; GP = group psychotherapy; CR = cognitive restructuring; RDC = research diagnostic criteria; Ham-D = Hamilton Depression Rating Scale; TCA = tricyclic antidepressant; C-BASP = cognitive behavioral analysis system of psychotherapy.

Three early dropouts from the two active treatments were omitted from analyses. Follow-up of a subsample ($n = 14$) at 6 months suggested the stable persistence of treatment effects.

Fennell and Teasdale (1982) treated five subjects meeting RDC for major depressive disorder who had a Hamilton Depression Rating Scale (Ham-D) (Hamilton 1960) score ≥ 15 (mean $= 23$) and BDI ≥ 20 (mean $= 31$), had been depressed from 18 months (less than the temporal criterion for dysthymic disorder) to 16 years, and who had failed to respond to an "adequate trial" (undefined) of antidepressant medication. Therapists with 3½ months of CBT training provided 20 sessions over 4 months. Improvements were "modest": the mean Ham-D score fell from 22.8 to 17.4 (BDI from 30.8 to 21.4) and only one subject clearly improved (BDI ≤ 9). The authors attributed lack of improvement to "patient characteristics" (i.e., to chronicity of depression).

Harpin et al. (1982) identified 12 subjects who reported chronic depression averaging 18 years in duration, who had an intake Ham-D ≥ 20 and had not responded to antidepressant medication. Subjects were alternately assigned to 10 weeks of twice-weekly CBT or to a waiting list control. Therapy focused on remediation of interpersonal difficulties; subjects also received 25 mg [sic] of tricyclic antidepressant daily. The six subjects receiving active treatment had a significant ($t = 2.37$, df $= 5$, $P < .05$) fall in Ham-D from 26.0 ± 6.4 to 16.3 ± 14.6, whereas Ham-D did not change in waiting list controls. The between-group difference in Ham-D change score was not statistically significant. At 6-month follow-up subjects who had received active treatment still had lowered anxiety, but Ham-D scores no longer differed significantly from pretreatment. Two of six treated patients showed major pre-post improvement on the Ham-D, and one maintained this at 6-month follow-up, whereas no control subjects improved.

Stravynski et al. (1991) reported treating six patients clinically diagnosed as having DSM-III dysthymic disorder with 15 hourly sessions of CBT. Two additional dysthymic subjects diagnosed as having narcissistic and dependent personality disorders were excluded. Independent raters observed "significant improvement" at termination and at 6-month follow-up; Ham-D fell from 23.7 ± 2.6 to 9.3 ± 1.8 posttreatment and 8.5 ± 9.8 at 6 months, and BDI fell from 26.3 ± 3.1 to 11.7 ± 4.5 posttreatment and 10.9 ± 8.9 at 6 months. Four subjects no longer met criteria for dysthymic disorder posttreatment. The authors suggested that responders had dysthymia with a discrete onset defined by a precipitating life event.

McCullough (1991) described treating 10 cases of DSM-III dysthymic disorder with his manualized Cognitive-Behavioral Analysis System of Psychotherapy (C-BASP), entailing 14–44 weekly sessions (mean $= 31 \pm 9.3$). Eight patients had double depression (J. McCullough, personal communication, April 1993). All reached termination criteria (BDI and Rotter Locus of Control Scale scores ≤ 10), and 9 patients remained in remission 2 years later. Of an original cohort of 20, 4 did not complete therapy, and the other 6 were unavailable for follow-up; following the author's methodology, their data were not evaluated (J. McCullough, personal communication, May 1993).

Mercier and colleagues (1992) treated 15 DSM-III dysthymic patients within a sample of patients with atypical depression. Three of 8 subjects with dysthymic disorder alone and 3 of 7 with double depression responded to a 12- to 16-week trial of standard CBT. All responders had been depressed 7 years or longer. Response upon completing CBT was defined as a Clinical Global Impression (McGlashan 1973) score of 1–2 (much or very much improved), indicating a major reduction in psychopathology and no need for additional treatment. Of all CBT responders, 69% maintained improvement over a 6-month follow-up that included four preplanned booster sessions; the rate of sustained remission among dysthymic patients is not stated.

Thase et al. (1994) compared 16-week treatments of 40 men with acute major depression to 22 with double depression ($n = 15$) or chronic major depression ($n = 7$). Chronically depressed patients responded more slowly and less completely. Although symptoms declined in both groups, with "similar rates of symptomatic change," only 27% of chronically depressed subjects, versus 55% of acutely depressed subjects, reached the criteria for remission (Ham-D < 7 on two consecutive ratings).

In summary, there have been eight reports of cognitive-behavioral treatments of dysthymic disorder or chronic major depression. Most treated small, idiosyncratic samples (e.g., inpatients, varying degrees of antidepressant nonresponse) and used varying outcome measures. None formally monitored therapist adherence to the psychotherapy protocol, and most reports (Harpin et al. 1982; McCullough 1991; Mercier et al. 1992; Stravynski et al. 1991) reflect the work of a single therapist. Most included some degree of follow-up assessment, an appropriate consideration for treatment of a chronic disorder. If results have not been dramatic, they do suggest that some dysthymic patients respond to brief cognitive therapies. Indeed, the cumulative response rate of 39% (see Table 2–2) approaches the efficacy reported in controlled trials of antidepressant medication. The scarcity of evidence, however, renders hopeful conclusions preliminary.

Interpersonal Psychotherapy

The National Institute of Mental Health (NIMH) Treatment of Depression Collaborative Research Program (Elkin et al. 1989; Sotsky et al. 1991) focused on treatment of major depression but did include subjects with double depression (RDC-defined major depression plus chronic minor depression or intermittent depressive disorder). Seventy-one (29.8%) such subjects were randomized to treatment with IPT, CBT, imipramine, or placebo, and 43 (26.7%) completed the trial. In exploratory analyses, double depression was associated with greater initial depressive severity and predicted poorer placebo response. Double depression predicted higher symptom severity at termination and incomplete response across treatment conditions. Chronicity and severity of mood disorder thus appeared to predict poorer outcome, although not lack of improvement, in standardized treatments for major depression.

IPT, like CBT, is a time-limited, manualized, psychotherapy that has demonstrated efficacy in controlled clinical trials for outpatient major depression and an increasing range of other diagnoses. The IPT therapist helps the patient recognize links between mood and current interpersonal experiences, focusing the therapy on one of four interpersonal problem areas: grief, role dispute, role transition, or interpersonal deficits (Klerman et al. 1984). Depression is explained as a medical illness rather than a personality defect, and the patient is given the sick role (Parsons 1951). IPT has shown benefit for treatment of acute depression (Klerman et al. 1984) as well as prophylaxis against recurrent major depression (Frank et al. 1990). Interpersonal approaches have been suggested to treat dysthymic disorder (Akiskal 1990; Cassano et al. 1990; Goldberg and Bridges 1990; Hirschfeld 1990; Weissman and Akiskal 1984) in recognition of the interpersonal difficulties dysthymic patients encounter. At Cornell we have developed a manual adapting IPT to dysthymic disorder (IPT-D), specifying adaptations including the diagnosis of dysthymic disorder within therapy as a novel form of interpersonal role transition (i.e., the transition out of chronic depression and into euthymia). Therapists are regularly supervised and monitored for treatment adherence.

Pilot data include three small series of subjects. In the first, Mason treated nine dysthymic subjects with IPT: five women who failed to respond to a vigorous desipramine trial, and four subjects who refused medication (Mason et al. 1993a). Their mean age was 37 ± 5.4 (standard deviation [SD]) years; most reported protracted dysthymic disorder (mean duration 22.4 ± 18.9 years, omitting the first 5 years of life). Subjects received 12.0 ± 4.9 sessions of IPT (range 3–16). Initial Ham-D scores for the group averaged 19.4 ± 5.0. Scores fell for all subjects; mean Ham-D at termination was 7.4 ± 3.8. When compared in quasiexperimental design with randomly chosen dysthymic subjects treated with desipramine, IPT response was equivalent to medication.

A separate project using IPT to treat depressed HIV-seropositive individuals included two dysthymic subjects. These white homosexual men, ages 47 and 32, reported lifelong depression. Despite the added stress of HIV infection, they improved on Ham-D from a mean 20.5 at intake to 5.0 at termination of IPT (12 and 16 sessions, respectively) (Markowitz et al. 1992b).

We continued IPT-D pilot work to test its replication with additional therapists. Two therapists completed treatment on six subjects, producing drops in Ham-D from 20.8 ± 6.4 (BDI 25.2 ± 9.5) at baseline to 8.5 ± 6.3 (BDI 12.7 ± 8.2) at acute termination (week 16). Responders are generally maintaining their gains when seen in monthly continuation sessions, with up to 2 years of follow-up.

Thus a total of 17 patients, including 7 who had failed vigorous desipramine trials, have received IPT from three therapists; none worsened, and 11 (65%) reached remission (Ham-D ≤ 8); overall mean Ham-D scores fell from 21.5 ± 4.4 at baseline to 7.4 ± 4.7 at acute termination. For IPT, as for CBT, outcome results are limited but encouraging.

Serial Treatment Data

The Columbia mood disorders group has raised interesting questions of treatment specificity: that is, whether patients unresponsive to one antidepressant modality may respond to another. Stewart and colleagues (1993) reported that a subset of CBT nonresponders from the Mercier et al. (1992) study responded to imipramine but not to placebo. Two pure dysthymic subjects and two double-depressive subjects who failed CBT responded to imipramine, whereas two double-depressive subjects randomized to placebo did not respond (J. Stewart, personal communication, April 1993).

The one responder in the Fennell and Teasdale (1982) study and two psychotherapy responders in the study by Harpin and colleagues (1982) had been preselected as medication nonresponders, albeit details of medication trials were not specified. In our studies, seven nonresponders to a 10-week trial of high-dosage desipramine improved with IPT. Although the numbers involved are small indeed, the results imply that medication and psychotherapy may serve complementary purposes in treating differing populations of dysthymic patients. If one approach does not work, the alternative may be worth trying.

Combined treatment might be expected to be a common prescription for these reputedly difficult patients, yet studies of combined treatment are still more limited than those of single modality. (They are also more complex to conduct.) In studies of acute major depression, combined pharmacotherapy and psychotherapy never has fared worse than either therapy alone (Manning et al. 1992).

Miller et al. (1985) found in an open trial that two of four treatment-refractory inpatients with DSM-III double depression responded to the combination of either CBT or social skills training (SST) (Becker et al. 1987) and assorted psychotropic medication (including antidepressants as well as neuroleptics in two cases). Psychotherapy was delivered 5 days per week after 2 weeks of inpatient assessment, with patients receiving a mean 28 sessions over a mean 22 weeks.

Becker and Heimberg (unpublished observations, 1987) reported preliminary results on 39 mildly symptomatic dysthymic subjects randomly assigned to SST or crisis-supportive psychotherapy and to nortriptyline or placebo. Patients received 16 weekly sessions followed by 2 biweekly sessions. Initial 17-item Ham-D mean was 10.9, declining to 4.5 at termination. Self-report and clinician ratings showed significant improvement for all four treatment conditions, without significant differences among them.

Waring et al. (1988) described 12 women meeting RDC for dysthymia [sic] randomized to 10 weeks of cognitive marital or supportive therapy and to doxepin (maximum 150 mg/day) or atropine placebo. All patients improved (mean Ham-D pretreatment, 14.5; posttreatment, 7.1; $P = .003$). Final results have not been reported for either the Becker et al. or the Waring et al. study.

A consortium of chronic depression researchers, in collaboration with a pharmaceutical company, is currently conducting a multisite, university-based study to compare the relative acute and maintenance efficacy of nefazodone, an atypical antidepressant medication, with a modified form of McCullough's C-BASP (J. P. McCullough, unpublished manuscript, 1992) and a combination of the two to treat patients with double and chronic major depression. At the time of this writing, the results of treatment had not yet been analyzed.

Finally, with support from the Nancy Pritzker Network, our research group at Cornell University Medical College has added a fourth treatment group, combined IPT-D plus the SSRI sertraline (Zoloft), as a 16-week treatment in our study of patients with dysthymic disorder.

The 1987 NIMH Workshop on Combined Medication and Psychotherapy in Depression concluded that discriminating between antidepressant effects of psycho- and pharmacotherapy is difficult because both treatments are so effective and because sample sizes in most studies have been small. Patients with chronic depression were deemed an ideal treatment population for differentiating combined and mode-specific treatment benefits of antidepressant therapies. The studies have yet to be done.

Discussion

As yet there have been no large, systematic controlled clinical trials of the psychotherapy of dysthymic disorder. Data from open trials are scarce but promising. Dysthymic disorder is coming more and more to resemble a lingering variant of acute major depression, which already has been shown to be responsive to antidepressant psychotherapy. As the two mood disorders converge, the case for testing the efficacy of psychotherapy in dysthymic disorder is strengthened. If, as antidepressant medication trials suggest, dysthymic patients are more difficult patients than those with acute major depression, there is more reason to seek clinical tools to treat them.

The limited available evidence suggests that, contrary to intuition, brief psychotherapies may effectively treat the chronic mood disorder of dysthymic disorder. In our experience, an advantage of brief therapy is the pressure it puts on both patient and therapist to work actively and to maintain high expectations. Diagnostic data do corroborate the psychoanalytic perception that "masochism" is common among dysthymic individuals; we found that 35% of 34 dysthymic subjects met SCID-II criteria for self-defeating personality disorder (Markowitz et al. 1992a). The question is whether such features imply a bad prognosis and whether they represent trait or chronic state. It would be unsurprising if longer term therapists, daunted by the grinding chronicity of dysthymic patients, were unwittingly to collude with the dysthymic disorder (Cooper 1985) by setting lower psychotherapeutic goals, thereby achieving lesser or slower results. High expectations, a medical model of mood disorder, a "here-and-now" focus on current issues, and the leverage of time-limited therapy may help to jostle patients out of their dysthymic rut. Once relieved of mood disorder they experience a great release, a second lease on life.

Clinical Recommendations

Current evidence supports the use of antidepressant medication as standard treatment for dysthymic disorder. Psychotherapy may prove a useful adjunct to medication (Markowitz 1993). Although efficacy data are limited, psychotherapy may nonetheless offer a reasonable monotherapy, particularly for patients who have not previously received mood-targeted psychotherapy or who refuse medication. Should dysthymic disorder not improve after months of aggressive treatment, however, antidepressant medication should be reconsidered. A developed therapeutic alliance and the recognition that psychotherapy is not alleviating symptoms may induce a patient who has previously refused medication to try it at this point.

Suggestions for Research Trials of Antidysthymic Psychotherapy

1. Use of time-limited, manualized psychotherapy.   Beyond its therapeutic advantages, brief psychotherapy has clear economic benefits and allows comparison with pharmacologic interventions. At least three brief therapies for dysthymic disorder have been codified in manuals: C-BASP (McCullough 1991; J. P. McCullough, unpublished manuscript, 1992), SST (Becker 1987), and IPT-D (the current volume). Standard CBT, which has been manualized for treatment of acute depression, appears to have some efficacy for dysthymic disorder as well. The latter three therapies have been used in studies circumscribing time and frequency of sessions.

2. Interpersonal focus.   A theme in the studies under review is how frequently psychotherapies tailored for dysthymic disorder seek to attack the interpersonal difficulties that are a hallmark of the disorder. This is obviously the focus of IPT, but Harpin et al.'s (1982) behavioral description is also congruent with an interpersonal approach: It provides SST in "interpersonal themes," including "refusing unreasonable requests, expressing positive feelings to another." That protocol involved significant others in cases where "the goal of training was to improve the interpersonal interaction and communication between the subject and significant other." SST (Becker 1987) similarly emphasizes interpersonal behavior and social perception. McCullough (1991; J. P. McCullough, unpublished manuscript, 1992), although using different language and a different conceptual approach, also focuses on "person^1 × person^2 interaction" as "the basic subject matter for psychotherapy" (1992, p. 9).

This convergence of treatments reflects the salience of interpersonal difficulties in dysthymic disorder and the need to address them in antidysthymic psychotherapy. Group or family therapy also might help dysthymic patients focus on interpersonal issues.

3. Serial design.   Initial controlled treatment trials should assess efficacy of psychotherapy compared with a standard reference treatment (i.e., antidepressant medication with a placebo or other control condition). Because psychotherapy and medication may treat different dysthymic populations, nonresponders to either active treatment might well be crossed over to an open trial of the alternative.

4. Continuation and maintenance treatment.   Given the chronicity of dysthymic disorder, and the risk of relapse and recurrence for mood disorders generally, ongoing treatment is probably warranted to maintain acute gains. In this matter psychotherapy does not differ from pharmacotherapy of dysthymic disorder. Our limited experience suggests that remitted dysthymic patients greatly appreciate monthly continuation sessions and use the time after acute treatment to consolidate IPT treatment gains. The need for ongoing treatment could be tested in a randomized discontinuation trial.

5. Combined treatment trials. Some readers may think it premature to compare combined with single modality therapy before the efficacy of psychotherapy for dysthymic patients has been conclusively demonstrated. Yet even if psychotherapy alone were not to show utility, it still might augment the benefits of antidepressant medication for medication responders (Klerman et al. 1994). "Postdysthymic" medication responders approach but may not attain community levels of social and vocational functioning, at least acutely (Friedman 1993; Markowitz et al. 1996). They may no longer appear personality-disordered (our first two IPT-D responders ceased to meet SCID-II criteria for personality disorder as well as for SCID-P dysthymia); yet, not knowing how to act socially, they may need and greatly benefit from psychotherapy (Markowitz 1993).

Combined pharmacopsychotherapy may prove optimal for many dysthymic patients. Psychotherapy has the advantage of empowering patients to prove to themselves that they can control their mood and their environment. Medication may provide faster relief and may offer surer prophylaxis against recurrence (cf. Frank et al. 1990).

6. Follow-up assessments. Because dysthymic disorder is by definition chronic, acute treatment outcome may be less meaningful than repeated assessment over a follow-up period of 6 months or longer. Follow-up assessment should therefore be included in antidysthymic outcome research.

Psychotherapy research in dysthymic disorder has received relatively little funding. NIMH has funded one pharmacotherapy study of dysthymic disorder; the research for which this manual was developed is the first psychotherapy study of dysthymic disorder funded by NIMH. The dearth of psychotherapy research on chronic depression partly reflects the relatively late development of research psychotherapies, which were initially, and reasonably, focused on acute depression. Dysthymic disorder itself has had a slippery reputation; although chronic suffering over decades may equal or outweigh the pain of more severe but briefer major depression (Wells et al. 1992), many clinicians and researchers seem to have judged dysthymic disorder with suspicion, as a "soft" diagnosis. The diagnostic system is biased by a tyranny of the acute, defining "major" depression by severity of current symptoms and relegating severity of *duration* to the "subsyndromal." Yet, paradoxically, chronicity of symptoms may daunt psychotherapists who treat dysthymic disorder.

Perhaps too great attention has been paid to the distinction between pure dysthymic disorder and double depression. Some studies (e.g., R. E. Becker, unpublished observations, 1987; Waring 1988) have foundered in the pursuit of "pure" dysthymic patients. Yet the DSM-IV field trials found that 79% of dysthymic patients eventually develop a major depression, qualifying for double depression (J. P. McCullough, unpublished manuscript, 1992). What may be a largely artifactual difference in severity criteria (Kocsis and Frances 1987) may hold less prognostic and diagnostic importance than the chronicity of mood disorder. The pure dysthymia/double-depression distinction should not be a barrier to research, albeit an issue to be controlled for in studies.

Given the public health significance of dysthymic disorder and the availability of treatment technology, the time is ripe to answer Weissman and Akiskal's proposal for antidysthymic psychotherapy trials.

Summary

Pharmacotherapy is the better proven, and psychotherapy, despite a long tradition, the less proven treatment for dysthymic disorder. Antidepressant medication makes a rapid and dramatic difference for many dysthymic individuals. Time-limited psychotherapies such as IPT and CBT also may be effective in lifting patients out of chronic depression in a matter of weeks, although there are a dearth of controlled treatment data. Even less is known about the combination of psychotherapy and pharmacotherapy.

Background Reading on
Dysthymic Disorder and Its Treatment

There are few general references on this condition. Readers interested in further background on dysthymic disorder may wish to consult the following texts:

Books

Burton SW, Akiskal HS (eds): Dysthymic Disorder. London, Gaskell, 1990
Kocsis JH, Klein DN (eds): Diagnosis and Treatment of Chronic Depression. New York, Guilford, 1995

Journals With Special Issues
Devoted to Dysthymic Disorder

Keller MB (ed): Mood disorders. Psychiatr Clin North Am 19:1–178, 1996
Kocsis JH, Klein DN (eds): Dysthymic disorder. Psychiatr Ann 23:617–624, 1993
Kocsis JH, Friedman RA, Markowitz JC, et al: Maintenance therapy for chronic depression: a controlled clinical trial of desipramine. Arch Gen Psychiatry 53:769–774, 1996
Thase ME, Fava M, Halbreich U, et al: A placebo-controlled, randomized clinical trial comparing sertraline and imipramine for the treatment of dysthymia. Arch Gen Psychiatry 53:777–784, 1996

SECTION 2
Interpersonal Psychotherapy of Dysthymic Disorder

People are always blaming their circumstances for what they are. I don't believe in circumstances. The people who get on in this world are the people who get up and look for the circumstances they want, and, if they can't find them, make them.

—George Bernard Shaw,
Mrs. Warren's Profession

CHAPTER 3
Overview of Interpersonal Psychotherapy

In regard to melancholics, conversation on the subject
of their despondency is found to be highly injudicious.

—Samuel Tuke,
Description of the Retreat

I say Live, Live, because of the sun,
The dream, the excitable gift.

—Anne Sexton,
"Live"

The late Gerald L. Klerman, M.D., Myrna M. Weissman, Ph.D., and their colleagues developed interpersonal psycho-therapy (IPT) as a time-limited, reliably reproducible psychotherapy of outpatients with acute major depression. IPT is loosely based on the theories of the interpersonal school of psychoanalysis (Sullivan 1953) and more specifically on available research on the influence of psychosocial factors in depression. Klerman and colleagues (1984) developed a treatment manual with which they and others trained therapists and demonstrated the efficacy of IPT for major depression in a series of controlled clinical trials (DiMascio et al. 1979; Elkin et al. 1989; Klerman et al. 1974; Weissman et al. 1979, 1981). Since then the research success of IPT has led to its adaptation and testing for other disorders and patient populations (Klerman and Weissman 1993; Markowitz 1995a; Weissman and Markowitz 1994). There is also an IPT book for patients (Weissman 1995). Until recently IPT had been almost solely a research intervention. Now attempts are being made—this book is one attempt—to help disseminate this relatively simple yet remarkably potent treatment.

IPT contains all the nonspecific factors conceded to be important to the efficacy of any psychotherapy (Frank 1971): *providing a setting and a ritual for treatment, a sympathetic, understanding listener, an affectively charged therapeutic alliance, an explanation for the patient's woes, therapeutic optimism, and success experiences*. In addition, IPT offers a medical model of depression as an illness, as part of a simple but believable case formulation that focuses the treatment on real life events, on what the patient can do to take control of his or her life situation and depressive episode.

Treatment Setting

The length of therapy is determined at the outset. For acute treatment this generally means a duration of 12–16 weekly sessions. Sessions generally last 50 minutes. The goal of this acute treatment is to treat the mood disorder (or other targeted syndrome), not to overhaul the patient's character. Acute treatment, when successful, may be followed by a (usually less intensive) separately negotiated continuation or maintenance treatment, still time limited and explicitly contracted.

The length of treatment reflects the development of IPT as a research psychotherapy to be compared with antidepressant medications in relatively brief trials. The length of treatment is somewhat arbitrary, representing a compromise between the typical 6–8 weeks of a pharmacotherapy trial, which seemed too short for psychotherapy, and a lengthier trial that would stretch beyond reason the duration of unhelpful pharmacotherapy. In fact, 12 or 14 or 16 weeks is generally sufficient to treat an episode of major depression or dysthymic disorder. If IPT (or any treatment) has not had an effect by the end of that time, the therapist should rethink the treatment and consider the many other options available for treating depression.

Treatment Ritual

The therapist quickly orients the patient to the ground rules of IPT. The focus is on the "here and now": that is, on what is going on in the patient's life at present and on life events or social interactions that may have contributed to the onset or perpetuation of the mood disorder. Moreover, the focus is on what the patient does and can do in the here and now, outside the office, far more than on what the patient thinks in the office. Sessions are opportunities to review the week's events and to plan responses for the future. In effect, IPT is coaching for real life. IPT does not generally address dreams, the transference, or the remote past, although it does seek to find and change dysfunctional patterns in relationships. The sessions are more structured and the therapist is more active than in typical psychodynamic psychotherapy (whatever "typical" may mean!), less so than in many cognitive or behavioral treatments.

Sympathetic, Understanding Listener

The role of the IPT therapist is to be the patient's ally, supporter, and coach. The therapist is optimistic and realistic, in contrast to the depressed patient's pessimistic stance. The therapist fosters a supportive, positive transference but does not address the transference in sessions. Rather, the therapist focuses on the patient's affect, on the connection of the patient's mood to events and situations in the patient's current life. The therapist elicits what in the current life situation is troubling the patient, what the patient might like to do to change that situation, and the options available to achieve that change. At the same time, the IPT therapist is not afraid to offer suggestions if the patient does not recognize important options on his or her own.

Affectively Charged Alliance

In the written descriptions of techniques that follow, IPT is likely to sound more behavioral than it is in actual practice. Therapy that works simply on an intellectualized level can be only superficial. In contrast, IPT uses focused interventions to help the patient address emotionally meaningful situations in his or her current life. The therapist underscores the affective valence of recent life reversals and problematic interpersonal relationships in the patient's life and then works as an expert, friendly guide to help the patient resolve these problems.

Explanation for the Patient's Woes

The fundamental concept of IPT is that depression does not occur in a vacuum but rather in a social context. When bad things happen, you feel bad. Conversely, when you feel depressed, you tend to mishandle your social role, to interact ineffectively, and so bad things are likely to happen. This can result in a vicious cycle; bad events lead to worsening mood, which in turn leads to further bad events.

Depression is considered a medical illness in IPT, and the therapist espouses a medical model. Scales such as the Hamilton Depression Rating Scale (Ham-D) (Hamilton 1960) and Beck Depression Inventory (Beck 1978) and diagnostic criteria sets from DSM-IV (American Psychiatric Association 1994) are used to reify the disorder. This helps to show the patient that the problem is not because of his or her idiosyncratic weakness, indolence, or evil, but rather is a recognizable, prevalent, and treatable medical condition.

Having derived the patient's interpersonal situation from a careful anamnesis, the therapist links this interpersonal problem to the newly diagnosed mood disorder in an explicit *formulation* (Markowitz and Swartz 1997). This is usually quite straightforward, as in the following:

> We've just diagnosed you as having an episode of major depression, which is a common and treatable medical illness. It seems to me that your depression has a lot to do with what's been happening in your life lately. Your symptoms seem to have started shortly after your husband died and you had trouble dealing with his death. This is not an uncommon way for depression to present—we call it complicated bereavement—and it's treatable.

It is important to underscore that IPT does not present a causal theory of depression—the etiology of depression is complex and multidetermined. But it is a pragmatic, convincing, and easily grasped explanation to many patients for why they are feeling so badly, and it raises the hope that the therapist can also help them to treat this newly diagnosed problem. The case formulation, linking the mood disorder to the interpersonal problem area, comes early in treatment, is discussed openly with the patient, and in fact provides the focus for the remainder of the course of therapy (Markowitz and Swartz 1997).

Therapeutic Optimism

Few therapies are based on therapeutic pessimism, so this topic may strike the reader as trivial. Yet few qualities are more important than optimism when dealing with a depressed patient, who almost by definition lacks it. And few therapies, in my experience, are more optimistic than IPT. Not only is the therapist's stance consciously encouraging and optimistic, but the therapist has good reason to hope for the best.

First, we know that depression is a highly treatable condition. The patient's pessimism is almost always unwarranted, no matter how difficult his or her actual life situation may be. Second, the therapist can trust in the efficacy of IPT not simply as a matter of training or ideological belief but based on solid research outcome data; we know that it works for most patients. Third, the therapist has good reason not to become discouraged. Each of the four interpersonal problem areas on which IPT can focus—grief, role dispute, role transition, and interpersonal deficits—has specific strategies and interventions on which the therapist can rely. Fourth, the therapy presents a simple but potent framework for the patient to understand his or her situation and effective tools for choosing and testing life options. Outcome depends on what the patient does outside the office rather than relying on the potency of an interpretation or inner change. The depressed patient who succeeds in changing his or her life situation—at a moment of greatest weakness and perceived incompetence—is almost bound to feel better, both because of the achievement itself and because of the improvement in life circumstances.

Success Experiences

This brings us to success experiences. Most therapies rely on success experiences, but usually these mean therapeutic breakthroughs in the office, during sessions. For depressed patients, and particularly those in a brief therapy, the more important goal is to achieve real life successes. From the start, the IPT therapist therefore encourages the patient to work on changing problematic situations, relationships, and interpersonal patterns outside the office. By the time an acute therapy ends, in 12 or 16 weeks, the patient not only may feel better but also may have altered his or her life situation and life course in impressive ways.

We have been particularly persuaded of the importance of this point in our work with depressed patients infected with human immunodeficiency virus (HIV) (Markowitz et al. 1992b, 1995). Here are young patients who know they have a lethal illness that has frequently devastated their interpersonal circles and that complicates their personal life trajectory and their relationships with others. One might well conclude that such patients should give up. But again, therapists should not negatively prejudge difficult situations; we have found that such patients, goaded by the time pressure of their illness, are often willing to make spectacular life changes in a matter of weeks. They live out their fantasies, move to new places, start new careers, begin better relationships—and their depression improves.

It is important that the therapist credit the patient for success experiences as they arise. The goal is to bolster the patient's self-esteem, not the therapist's; in any case, in IPT it is easy to determine that the patient really deserves the credit. The patient has determined which goals to pursue in changing his or her interpersonal environment. More importantly, the patient is the one who has left the office and dealt with life situations to achieve the success experiences. The therapist can feel gratified by therapeutic success and take pride in being an able coach, but he or she should underscore the patient's role in resolving the interpersonal problem and in thereby treating the depression.

Why does IPT work? The emphasis of IPT research to date has been on outcome research, not on its process. (This reflects the late Gerald L. Klerman's belief that process therapy should not be undertaken until one knows that the therapy has an effect.) One study showed that maintaining a consistent interpersonal focus in therapy sessions was associated with efficacy (Frank et al. 1991a). My own feeling is that IPT is an eclectic therapy that has the solid basic elements common to many therapies. In addition, IPT provides a wonderful rationale for depression and its treatment to any patient *who has had difficult life events*. This, I think, explains its efficacy with depressed HIV-positive patients. The clean simplicity of the treatment and the sharpness of its focus make it "user friendly" for both patient and therapist. Because of the research outcome data, the IPT therapist has good reason to stay confident, and the therapist's pragmatic optimism is infectious; once it is translated into the patient's success experiences, it is almost sure to lead to a good outcome.

Basic Principles of IPT

The best and most detailed description of IPT can be found in the original manual (Klerman et al. 1984). To provide the broad outlines, IPT has three phases: beginning, middle, and end. From the start, the program is simple, pragmatic, and organized to help the patient understand his or her situation and deal with depressive symptoms.

All depends on the nonetiological axiom that life events (and the social environment) affect mood and that mood conversely influences social functioning and response to one's environment. This is common sense; we know that good events make you feel good, bad events make you feel bad. Everyone knows this—except depressed patients, who often turn inward and blame themselves, rather than looking to their environment. On being reminded of this by the therapist, patients generally recognize that their perspective has been warped by depression. Thus this central interpersonal tenet not only serves as a fulcrum for understanding and battling depression, its explanation also provides an opportunity for psychoeducation about depression. IPT offers patients the opportunity to solve a difficulty in their interpersonal functioning and simultaneously to relieve depression.

As one of my trainees put it, "IPT is less interested in how you got into the depression than in how you can get out of it." Or, to be slightly more precise, IPT focuses on psychosocial history only to determine precipitants to and avenues out of the depressive episode.

The Three Phases of Treatment

Initial Phase

The first phase of IPT usually comprises one to three sessions, depending on the efficiency of the therapist, the patient's capability as a historian, and the obviousness of the interpersonal focus of the therapy. The first phase has three major purposes: 1) to diagnose the disorder, if any, 2) to set the framework for the treatment to follow, and 3) to provide initial relief. This may sound like a great deal to accomplish in just a few sessions but is in fact possible to do without rushing the patient. Specific tasks of the initial phase are listed in Table 3–1.

Diagnostic Tasks

Depression. The IPT therapist *diagnoses depression as a medical illness.* Thus what the patient often has perceived as a personal weakness is instead identified as a common and treatable medical illness. Klerman and colleagues call this "giv[ing] the syndrome a name" (1984, pp. 73, 83). In doing so, the therapist is beginning the psychoeducation about depression, which is an important feature of the treatment. DSM-IV and depression rating scales may be used to help the patient recognize depression as a well-defined clinical entity. The rating scales are helpful change measures; when repeated serially over the course of treatment, they can help both patient and therapist to quantify the outcome of their work.

Table 3–1.   Tasks of the initial IPT sessions

---

1. Diagnostic
   a. Diagnose depression as a medical illness
   b. Anamnesis including interpersonal inventory
   c. Determine interpersonal problem area
   d. Interpersonal formulation
      • Link medical diagnosis of depression to interpersonal problem area
   e. Consider need for medication
2. Framing treatment
   a. Interpersonal, "here and now" focus
      • What does the patient want?
      • What options does the patient have?
   b. Sick role
   c. Activity and socialization
   d. Psychoeducation
   e. Therapeutic alliance—agreement on the formulation
   f. Treatment contract; logistics
3. Therapeutic
   a. Psychoeducation
   b. Instilling hope

Source.   Reprinted with permission from Klerman GL, Weissman MM, Rounsaville BJ, et al.: *Interpersonal Psychotherapy of Depression.* New York, Basic Books, 1984.

Interpersonal diagnosis.   In taking a careful psychiatric history, the IPT therapist takes an *interpersonal inventory:* a catalogue of the patient's key relationships, with an eye to the patient's capacity for intimacy and also to self-destructive recurring relationship patterns. Although the IPT therapist will ask about past relationships to look for patterns and vulnerabilities, the focus is on current relationships and particularly on recent changes in relationships that might yield an interpersonal focus for treatment. The therapist looks for areas of nonreciprocal expectations: situations in which the patient expects one thing from others, who themselves have different expectations of the relationship. What does the patient want from relationships? What are the strengths and the weaknesses of relationships that the patient has had to date? What are the limits to the patient's repertoire of interpersonal interactions?

Determining the problem area. In collecting the interpersonal inventory, the therapist may discover problematic recent life changes that can be temporally related to the onset of the mood disorder. These problems are classified within one of four interpersonal problem areas: *grief* (complicated bereavement), *role disputes*, *role transitions*, and *interpersonal deficits*. These broad problem areas derive from the available research findings on psychosocial aspects of depression at the time IPT was developed.

If, for example, the patient reported the death of a significant other, the therapist would explore how the patient had handled that loss. What had been the relationship between the patient and the deceased? Was the patient able to grieve? Difficulties in this area would suggest complicated bereavement as an interpersonal focus for the treatment to follow. In taking the history, the therapist should carefully rule out covert interpersonal problem areas, arriving at a clear focus that is likely to make sense to the patient.

Because patients often have more than one such problem area, choosing the most salient among them is an important aspect of the early phase. The therapist hopes to find one of the first three problem areas (grief, role dispute, or role transition) because they imply a recent life change, the material on which IPT capitalizes. Failing this, the therapist falls back on the default category of interpersonal deficits, which implies that the patient has had no recent life change and probably has a paucity of relationships. If more than two interpersonal problem areas exist, the therapist generally focuses on the one or two that have the highest affective valence to the patient. To have more than two such foci risks confusing the therapeutic field for both patient and therapist (Markowitz and Swartz 1997). It is best to keep things simple.

Interpersonal formulation. Once having determined the interpersonal problem area, the therapist offers the patient an interpersonal formulation that links it to the medical diagnosis. This provides the therapeutic focus for the remainder of the treatment.

> You have a major depression, which as we've discussed is a medical illness, and a treatable one. One way to treat it is with medication; another is with psychotherapy.
>
> It seems to me that your depression began when you began to get into struggles with your husband and your marriage seemed to go sour. We call this a role dispute. One way to treat your depression is a brief psychotherapy called interpersonal psychotherapy, which has been proven in research studies to help depression. IPT works by helping you to see the connection between what's going on in your life and how you feel. My sense is that if you can understand and do something to resolve your role dispute with your husband, you'll not only help your marriage but also relieve your depression. Does that make sense to you?

Thus in the interpersonal formulation the therapist offers the patient two potential benefits of the brief therapy: resolution of the interpersonal problem and remission of the depressive syndrome. The therapist needs the patient's formal agreement on the problem area because this will be the subsequent focus of treatment; if they do not agree, treatment is likely to go awry. Patients usually do agree with formulations, because they are simple and intuitively reasonable. In the rare circumstance that the patient disagrees, the therapist would propose an alternative formulation on which the two can agree. Once they mutually accept a formulation, IPT proceeds into its middle, and main, phase.

Differential therapeutics.　　Early in the evaluation process the therapist should consider, and discuss with the patient, the differential therapeutics of depression— an area about which we as yet know too little (Frances et al. 1984). Should the patient be treated with antidepressant medication, psychotherapy, or a combination? If psychotherapy, which form is preferable?

The patient's treatment history is often helpful in determining the best treatment options. Patient preference also plays an important role in determining treatment. Two factors that should not be important determinants of the prescription of therapy are 1) the limits imposed by insurance and managed care and 2) the ideological beliefs of the therapist (Klerman 1991).

The decision to prescribe medication instead of or in combination with psychotherapy should depend in part on the severity of the illness. Immobilizing neurovegetative symptoms of depression may render the patient too anergic to participate in psychotherapy, at least until antidepressant medication begins to take effect. High risk of suicide also argues for the use of antidepressant medication, which works more quickly than psychotherapy. Delusional depression should be treated with electroconvulsive therapy (ECT) or combined antidepressant and neuroleptic medications; IPT was not developed and has never been tested for the treatment of psychotic depression.

Patients who have had few life events and have strong ruminations—those likely to fall into the interpersonal deficits category of IPT—might do better in cognitive-behavior therapy (Sotsky et al. 1991).

Framing the Therapy

Interpersonal, "here-and-now" focus.　　Many patients bring preconceptions of therapy to the treatment. Influenced by media portrayals of psychotherapy or by their own previous treatments, they are likely to have little idea of what their role in IPT needs to be. The IPT therapist explains that treatment will focus on *what is currently happening in interpersonal relationships in the patient's life*, on *what the patient wants to happen*, and especially on *what options the patient has to achieve his or her desired goals*. Treatment will center on what happens outside the office more than on what happens within it. IPT sessions are an opportunity to determine the patient's desires and options, to prepare the patient to test those options, and to assess the results of the previous week's experience.

Sick role.   IPT therapists give their patients the sick role. As defined by Parsons (1951), this role has both privileges and responsibilities. One benefit of the sick role—important to depressed patients—is that *they are excused for being depressed. Having an illness is not your fault.* Helpful comparisons may be made to other medical problems:

> You wouldn't blame yourself for having diabetes or high blood pressure. These, too, can run in families and can be treated with both medication and behavioral interventions.

> If you had a broken leg, you wouldn't expect to run in a marathon, right? Or if you had pneumonia, you wouldn't blame yourself for feeling too sick to go to work. If you're really feeling too depressed to go to work tomorrow, that shows you're really ill, and you shouldn't blame yourself. I'd encourage you to be as active as you can, but if you can't go, you're excused.

Although this absolution from blame might seem to raise the risk of regression during the therapy, several factors prevent patients from regressing during IPT. One is the guilt that depressed patients feel when they are inactive. Another is gentle pressure from the therapist for activity and socialization during the treatment. A third is the time pressure of the time-limited format; the patient knows that time is precious and dares not regress.

The sick role shifts patients' blame from themselves to an illness, which the therapist blames for their suffering. This reconceptualization helps make symptoms that patients had considered part of themselves into ego-dystonic manifestations of a disease.

The other aspect of the sick role is the responsibility it entails: to be a good patient and to work in IPT at solving the interpersonal problem area, thereby treating the depression. The patient must come to sessions, learn the connection between mood and life events, and plan and enact strategies to improve his or her life situations. Although IPT patients are not assigned formal homework, the whole thrust of the therapy informs them of the need to make changes in their interpersonal situation. The ultimate resolution of the sick role is to recover the healthy role.

Shifting self-blame is an important issue for overly critical depressed patients. Dysthymic patients are particularly prone to self-blame (cf. Table 1–2). In general, the IPT therapist refocuses blame either on the illness of depression or on the interpersonal situation (problem area) in which the patient finds him- or herself.

Activity and socialization.   Depressed patients tend to withdraw socially and retreat inwardly, frequently spending much of their time alone or even lying in bed. These are natural tendencies when one is depressed, yet they tend to worsen the depression. Thus isolated, the depressed individual has plenty of time to ruminate about his or her worthlessness and laziness. The patient who lies in bed thinking, "I'm useless, I'm not doing anything" is in some measure correct.

Activity is therefore prescribed in most treatments for depression. This prescription must take into account the depressed patient's limited energy and initiative and the risk of social failures that might compound depressed feeling. But activity does have at least mild antidepressant benefit. Activity distracts the patient from ruminations. It contradicts the patient's sense of being unable to do anything. And there is the possibility that, while engaged in an activity, the patient may actually have a good time or, still better, wander into a good event such as a new friendship or a job opportunity. Brown and Harris (1978) have described the importance of such "fresh starts" in recovery from depression. Fresh starts are unlikely to occur while the patient is lying abed.

Beyond the general importance of activity in countering depression, mobilizing the patient to social interaction is critical to IPT. Because the therapy focuses on what has happened in the patient's life between sessions, a week spent in bed strips the next session of the interpersonal material on which the therapy works.

Psychoeducation.   In keeping with the medical model of depression as an illness, IPT encourages the patient to become an expert on depression and its treatment. The emphasis on an illness absolves the patient of personal blame, in effect normalizing the patient's situation by medically pathologizing it. The knowledge that there are many effective treatments for depression can only imbue hope. It is important to remind patients that their hopelessness is a common depressive symptom—that is why it is on the Hamilton Depression Rating Scale. Reading the IPT literature, including the IPT patient book (Weissman 1995), may encourage patients that they are involved in a treatment of proven efficacy. Even if IPT should not help them, they can learn of the many effective alternative treatments. All this is in keeping with the IPT emphasis on exploring one's options.

Therapeutic alliance.   In the first sessions of IPT, while diagnosing the patient and setting the framework for the rest of the treatment, the therapist provides the patient with support, encouragement, and reassurance, thereby building a therapeutic alliance. Both therapist and patient are active participants in the treatment. The alliance is most obviously forged when the therapist presents the interpersonal formulation for the patient's agreement. Once they agree, they can proceed into the middle phase as a team.

Treatment contract.   Therapist and patient need to agree not only on the focus of therapy but also on its length and other logistics. The patient should understand the timing and length of the treatment (generally 12–16 weeks for acute therapy) and of individual sessions (usually 50 minutes).

> If you agree [with the interpersonal formulation], I'd like to suggest that we meet once a week for the next 12 weeks to focus on your role dispute [or other interpersonal problem area]. As we work on your interpersonal problem area, and you solve it, your depression should get better as well.

This is also the opportunity for therapist and patient to discuss fees, handling emergencies, and other contingencies of treatment. The goal is to keep everything clear and straightforward from the start.

Initial Relief

The initial phase of IPT necessarily concentrates on the development of a formulation and a framework more than on treatment per se. Nonetheless, the depressed patient notes the therapist's assurances and reassurances, the organized approach to treatment, and the clear, intuitively reasonable explanation of the connection between mood and social environment. Preliminary discussion of the patient's wishes and options is also encouraging. The therapist works from the start to offer hope and education about depression.

> Depression is an illness psychiatrists *like* to see. Not because we like to see people suffering—and I know you're suffering a great deal from your depressive illness—but because it's very treatable. Nothing in medicine is 100% guaranteed, but we have an excellent chance of helping you get out of this depression in the next weeks.

All these maneuvers have a cumulative effect. We have found that depression scores often drop by the end of the first session or two of IPT. The improvement represents, in a sense, a tentative sense of hope and reassurance on the patient's part, a positive placebo effect due to IPT. This relief may be only transient; the patient's willingness to try to believe in the treatment may vanish if an effective approach is not forthcoming. But at the very least it provides momentum for the therapy to proceed into its middle phase.

Middle Phase

This phase, the heart of the treatment, stretches from the agreement on an interpersonal focus until the last few sessions, which are a termination phase. During the middle phase, therapist and patient focus on one or sometimes two of the four IPT interpersonal problem areas:

- Grief (complicated bereavement)
- Role dispute
- Role transition
- Interpersonal deficits

Each of these problem areas has a distinct set of goals and strategies (Klerman et al. 1984). Yet the approaches to their treatment overlap significantly, and they rely on both common sense and a rationale based on psychosocial research on depression.

The Four Problem Areas

The four interpersonal problem areas will be covered in greater detail in the following chapter. In each case, the interpersonal situation is linked to the diagnosed mood disorder.

Grief

Grief is a normal emotion, not a psychiatric disorder. It has long been recognized, however, that people who have difficulty grieving, particularly when faced with an ambivalent or repeated loss, are prone to developing a depressive episode (Freud 1917). Thus *complicated bereavement* has long been recognized as a subtype of mood disorder. In IPT, grief requires that a person significant to the patient has actually died. Other, symbolic losses, such as the loss of an ideal or expectation (e.g., realizing you will never attain a long-sought goal such as promotion to a desired job) are treated in IPT as role transitions.

The goals of treating complicated bereavement are straightforward: to help the patient 1) to grieve appropriately and, having started this mourning, 2) to find new activities and relationships to substitute for the loss (cf. Table 4–2).

Role Dispute

Role disputes are significant struggles with a significant other in the patient's current interpersonal environment. The significant other may be a spouse, child, other family member, friend, enemy, boss, co-worker, etc. This category reflects research linking difficult relationships to episodes of depression in women (Paykel et al. 1969; Rounsaville et al. 1979; Weissman and Paykel 1974). The goals are to help the patient understand the nature of the dispute and its importance in relation to the depression, to determine whether the dispute is at an impasse, and to help the patient develop strategies to resolve the dispute.

Role Transition

This broad category includes any major life change: getting engaged, married, separated, or divorced; becoming a parent or having a child leave the home; getting hired, promoted, demoted, or fired; developing a serious illness, etc. Although most people feel some anxiety when faced with life changes, the majority survive such changes without developing depression. People who are vulnerable, however, may develop a depressive episode in the context of such stress. They tend to perceive their situations as hopelessly chaotic. They look back to the past as a golden age while seeing the present and future as miserable.

Goals of treating a role transition include helping the patient: 1) to mourn and accept the loss of the old role, 2) to regard the new role as more positive, and 3) to build self-esteem by developing a sense of mastery over demands of the new role (cf. Table 4–4).

Interpersonal Deficits

Patients with interpersonal deficits are chronically socially isolated; they have trouble making or sustaining relationships. The goals of treatment are to reduce the patient's social isolation and to encourage the formation of new relationships.

Several factors make this the least desirable of the four problem areas to use. First, this is a default category for patients who do not fit any of the three other categories (i.e., nothing has recently occurred in their lives that can be linked to the onset of their mood disorder). Second, this absence of social connection implies a lack of social skills; these patients have great difficulty in functioning in the arena where

IPT works. It is more difficult to develop a therapeutic alliance and to work with these patients. They often have schizoid or paranoid features or meet criteria for these axis II personality disorders. Finally, this IPT interpersonal problem area is the least theoretically developed. Thus, although this interpersonal problem area defines a more difficult to treat subset of depressed patients generally, it also may be the area where IPT does least well (Sotsky et al. 1991). Nonetheless, the therapist should not abandon hope; patients often can be successfully treated with this approach.

IPT Techniques

Beginning the Session

Regardless of the interpersonal focus of treatment, every IPT session after the first follows a characteristic pattern. The therapist begins each session with the question, "How have things been since we last met?" This deceptively simple question illustrates the bluntly brilliant approach of Klerman, Weissman, and colleagues. For one thing, it focuses the patient's attention on the immediate past, the interval between sessions. Next, it tends to elicit one of two responses: a description of either a mood or an event. In either case, it provides an opportunity for the therapist to help the patient recognize a link between mood and event.

If the patient reports a mood ("I had a terrible week, I've been feeling awful"), the therapist wants to know

> What happened in the last week that might have contributed to your feeling so bad? . . . You said you felt worse after Tuesday; was there something that happened just before then?

If, on the other hand, the patient reports an event ("Well, this was the week of the office party"), the complementary question would be

> And how did that go? . . . How did you feel there? And afterwards?

Thus the opening question both frames the context of the session in the patient's immediate past and underscores the thematic connection between the patient's mood and life events.

This opening gambit does still more. If the patient's answer leads to an emotionally laden event, the therapist explores it further. (If not, the therapist tries again to find such an event or mood shift in the previous week.) Gathering specific details of an interpersonal interaction clarifies the patient's behaviors and emotional reactions in that situation. The therapist requests as nearly as possible a verbatim recounting of the crucial event (i.e., communication analysis). If the situation went well, the therapist praises the patient for handling a difficult encounter despite feeling depressed and congratulates the patient on his or her success. If the situation ended poorly, the therapist helps the patient recognize why that might have happened (e.g., not really expressing a need to a spouse, difficulty in expressing anger) and to learn from mistakes. Having identified the problem, therapist and patient might consider alternative strategies and role play them in the session until the patient feels comfortable trying them out in "real life." Thus the initial question can bring to light important interpersonal material.

Moreover, the incident that therapist and patient identify typically leads into the interpersonal problem area (grief, role dispute, role transition, interpersonal deficits) that they have agreed is central to the therapy. If a patient in a role dispute reports having had a good or bad week, it is a fair bet that the report has something to do with the role dispute that is central to the patient's life. Hence beginning with a description of mood and an affectively laden incident leads the patient from a particular event to the general problem area. Focusing on an incident to which the patient attaches emotion minimizes the chance that this discussion of the focal interpersonal problem area will be intellectualized and emotionally distanced.

Other techniques

IPT therapists encourage patients to describe their feelings about current life situations. They validate the patient's sense that these are painful events, not to be trivialized:

> Yes, that must have been terrible when your child died. . . . Losing a child is probably one of the worst stresses anyone suffers.

But IPT is not simply a matter of catharsis. In addition to evoking affect, the IPT therapist also works to help the patient find solutions to the interpersonal dilemma:

> Now that this has happened, what can you do to repair your situation? What would you like to happen? What would help you to feel better?

Having determined *what the patient wants*, the therapist helps the patient to *explore available options to achieve that wish*. Most depressed patients initially state that they have no options—a statement so obviously untrue that it again provides a helpful opportunity for psychoeducation about depression. A number of patients have told me, at the end of therapy, that recognizing that there always are options—even when depression makes it hard to see them—was one of the most valuable aspects of IPT.

Clarification and *communication analysis* are also important tools. Hearing a patient relate an interchange with a significant other, and asking about the patient's emotional responses to it, may alert the therapist to dysfunctional patterns in the patient's behavioral repertoire. Clarification restructures the patient's story so that the patient can better understand an incident that he or she has just related. This is particularly useful for pointing out contrasts between how patients envision their own role in a situation and how they in fact behave.

> You've said that you don't like it when there are secrets in relationships, and yet here you seem to be keeping a secret from your husband.

or

> You say you were angry at your colleague at work, but it's hard for me to hear how that came out in this situation.

Clarification can be used to crystallize interpersonal patterns for the patient.

In communication analysis, the therapist elicits a blow-by-blow, insofar as possible, verbatim description of an interpersonal interchange. In addition to determining the exact words that the patient and significant others have used, the therapist inquires about the patient's emotional responses to each stage of the encounter, and the tone of voice the patient used. This is often valuable for determining contradictions in the patient's view of these interchanges and of his or her role in them. For example, many depressed patients have enormous difficulty in communicating their anger.

> You say you were angry, and we agree that there's good reason to be angry about this situation. Yet what you told your husband was, "You hurt my feelings." To me that sounds hurt, not angry. What do you think?

Gently pointing out such discrepancies to the patient, and brainstorming with the patient, may help the latter determine better alternatives to such situations.

Communication analysis often leads to role playing. *Role playing* becomes an excellent preparation for new alternatives. The therapist can play the significant other, with the patient testing out a new role for him- or herself. If an angry patient has said nothing, or something more along the lines of "You hurt my feelings!" than "I'm angry at the way you've been treating me!" practice in the office is often crucial. Feedback from the therapist can help the patient to tune words, tone of voice, facial expression, and other emotional semiotics to the task at hand. It is a fair bet that if the patient cannot act out a behavior with the therapist in a session, the patient will not be able to do it with a significant other. With practice in role play, however, the patient may have a chance to significantly alter a key interpersonal relationship in life beyond the office. The therapeutic relationship is not used to interpret the transference. Rather, the therapist acts as a supportive ally, fostering a positive, supportive transference. In the instance of a patient with interpersonal deficits, who has no other social interactions, the therapist sometimes may be forced to address the therapeutic relationship as the only available interpersonal material. Yet even here the emphasis is on a real-life, here-and-now interaction.

> We've agreed that we're going to work on the discomfort you feel in social situations. It's important that you tell me here if I say something that angers you or makes you anxious. I hope I don't, but if I do we should talk about it, so that we can figure out what the difficulty is. That may help you with other relationships you can form outside our meetings.

The expectation is always that practice in the therapeutic relationship will allow the patient to build other relationships outside the office. Because IPT is time limited and often brief, the therapist emphasizes the importance of outside, lasting relationships rather than the temporary one in the office.

Termination Phase

As the final weeks of treatment approach, the patient usually has improved. Not only has the depressive episode resolved, but the patient often has made dramatic changes in his or her interpersonal environment en route. The patient thinks the therapist and the therapy are great; the therapist feels equally positive about the patient. Both often think: Why break up a good team? We could keep on going—there are plenty of other things we could work on. . . .

They have arrived at the moment psychotherapists probably handle least capably: ending therapy. But it is important to remember that IPT began with a contract to treat the depression, not to address all of the patient's problems. When the goal of euthymia has been achieved, it is time to prepare the patient for ending the acute treatment. As with much else in IPT, the therapist makes this change of phase explicit (see Table 3–2).

Table 3–2. Tasks of the final sessions

1. Explicit discussion of the end of acute treatment
2. Termination as a graduation from therapy
3. Acknowledgment of termination as a time of potential sadness
4. Review of the patient's accomplishments in treatment
   a. Crediting the patient
5. Discussion of depression
   a. The risk of recurrence
   b. The signs, symptoms, and treatability of depression
   c. The patient's likely areas of interpersonal vulnerability
6. For partial responders or nonresponders
   a. Avoiding guilt
   b. Exploring other therapeutic options

Source.   Reprinted with permission from Klerman GL, Weissman MM, Rounsaville BJ, et al.: *Interpersonal Psychotherapy of Depression.* New York, Basic Books, 1984.

The therapist congratulates the patient on his or her success in their work while conceding that termination is potentially bittersweet. On the one hand, and mainly, it is a victory and success for the patient; termination is a graduation from treatment, an assumption of a healthier role. On the other hand, it is often sad to leave the university, sad that the therapy team will have to part.

> It's always hard to break up a good team—and we've been working so well together! But you've done such a good job in resolving your role transition [or other interpersonal problem area] that you're not depressed anymore, so it's time to remember that we'll be stopping in 3 weeks.

If the patient does feel sad about stopping, this emotion provides a useful opportunity to help the patient distinguish the pathological symptom complex of a mood disorder from the normal, appropriate sadness of ending a relationship. The patient will by now know that changes in the social environment have effects on affect.

Having reminded the patient that the end is approaching, the therapist reviews all that has happened—which is generally considerable—in the course of a relatively brief therapy. This includes a review of the basic principles of IPT (i.e., mood affects events and vice versa), what the patient has done to resolve the interpersonal problem area(s), and the concomitant improvement in depressive symptomatology.

The pair also reviews the symptoms of depression, the considerable risk of relapse and recurrence, and the range of available treatment options. And they consider the patient's particular interpersonal vulnerabilities, factors that might put the patient at risk for another episode of depression in the future. Although IPT does not pretend to change character in the course of 12–16 weeks, IPT patients often do gain awareness of their interpersonal patterns and develop new social skills (Weissman et al. 1981), at least smoothing the rough edges of character in key social situations. Patient and therapist thus may be able to anticipate and prepare for future difficulties.

Of course, not every patient will respond to IPT. Even patients whose depression does not fully remit, however, rarely leave empty-handed. In my experience, many have succeeded in solving their interpersonal problem area, but their symptoms have not, or have only partially, improved. This represents a failure of IPT's theoretical mechanism; that is, resolution of the interpersonal problem area is supposed to resolve depressive symptoms.

When patients have made an effort in therapy, it is crucial that they not leave blaming themselves as failures—as depressed patients have a tendency to do. In such cases, the therapist should blame the therapy instead:

> It's not you who have failed, but the therapy! The therapy said that solving your interpersonal problem would lead to the clearing of your depression. You did what you were supposed to do, it's the therapy that hasn't. I think you've done a really good job, and I want to make sure that you don't blame yourself for IPT's failure. Luckily, there are lots of other ways to treat depression.

Nonresponders are often pleased to see that they have been able to accomplish important interpersonal goals and to develop new skills *despite* being depressed. Some patients who refused to take medication before the course of IPT have gained sufficient understanding of mood disorders and trust of the therapeutic alliance that they are then willing to try psychopharmacologic options. In dealing with a patient who has not responded to IPT, the therapist should in any case stress the idea of continuing to explore treatment options. The optimistic exploration of the many available treatments for depression, and the empirically based assumption that depression is generally treatable, follow naturally from the IPT context.

Continuation Treatment

Because major depression frequently recurs, and the risk of recurrence increases with the number of previous episodes (Keller et al. 1992), clinical judgment may reasonably dictate the utility of ongoing therapy after the success of an acute treatment. Alone among time limited psychotherapies, IPT has been tested and has demonstrated efficacy as both a continuation treatment (Klerman et al. 1974) and a 3-year maintenance treatment (Frank et al. 1990; see Weissman 1994). Dosing strategies (i.e., the frequency of sessions) have yet to be tested for ongoing IPT treatment; the landmark Pittsburgh study found benefits for a monthly maintenance form of IPT (IPT-M) in treating patients at extremely high risk for relapse and recurrence (Frank et al. 1990, 1991a). If a patient has done well in acute IPT and the therapist deems ongoing treatment appropriate, the therapist still should mark the termination of acute treatment and graduation to a new phase. Patient and therapist should agree on a new time frame and frequency of treatment and on appropriate new goals for that treatment—namely, to prevent relapse and recurrence of the mood disorder.

Research on IPT

Part of the therapist's confidence in IPT derives from its testing in controlled trials of outcome research. Several studies have demonstrated the efficacy of IPT in treating patients with major depression (DiMascio et al. 1979; Elkin et al. 1989; Klerman et al. 1974; Weissman et al. 1979, 1981) as well as in various subpopulations of depressed patients: geriatric (Sloane et al. 1985), adolescent (Moreau et al. 1991; Mufson et al. 1993), HIV positive (Markowitz et al. 1992b, 1995), and primary care (Schulberg et al. 1993, 1996).

The most ambitious acute treatment study to date is the multisite National Institute of Mental Health Treatment of Depression Collaborative Research Program. This program randomly assigned 250 depressed outpatients to 16 weeks of imipramine (IMI), IPT, cognitive-behavior therapy (CBT), or placebo (PLA) treatment (Elkin et al. 1989). Subjects who received either IMI or PLA pills also received "clinical management" (CM) (Fawcett et al. 1987), which included a biochemical rationale for why the medication should work, and warm, doctorly reassurance. Most subjects completed at least 15 weeks or 12 treatment sessions. This study was the first to directly compare IPT and CBT and to test the treatments for depression at sites away from where they had been developed.

Because the PLA/CM condition helped many patients, there was no overall difference among the four conditions (Elkin et al. 1989). Less symptomatic patients—those who had an initial Ham-D score of less than 20—improved equally in all four treatments. Among more severely depressed patients (initial Ham-D > 20), however, post hoc analyses did find differences among therapies. IMI/CM produced the most rapid response and was most clearly superior to PLA/CM in efficacy. IPT had the lowest attrition and was also superior to PLA/CM. On several outcome measures, IPT and IMI/CM were comparable, and superior to PLA/CM, whereas CBT, finishing a distant third, was not statistically separable from any of the other conditions.

A naturalistic follow-up study found considerable evidence of relapse 18 months after treatment (Shea et al. 1992). Because IPT and IMI/CM had been relatively successful in helping patients reach acute remission, they also had more patients at risk for relapse. Among patients who had recovered by the end of the 16-week treatment study, relapse over the 18-month follow-up was 36% for CT, 33% for PLA/CM, 33% for IPT, and 50% for IMI/CM (medication was also stopped at the end of the trial). These findings confirm that acute therapy does not provide lasting prophylaxis against a recurrent illness and argue for the use of maintenance therapy for many depressed patients.

Because of its success in research studies, IPT has been included in national (Karasu et al. 1993; U.S. Department of Health and Human Services 1993a, 1993b, 1993c, 1993d) and international guidelines as a treatment for mood disorders. Its success in treating mood disorders has also led to its expansion to other forms of psychopathology (Klerman and Weissman 1993), including bulimia (Fairburn et al. 1991, 1993; Wilfley et al. 1993) and, less successfully, substance abuse (Carroll et al. 1991; Rounsaville et al. 1983). IPT may even have efficacy for patients with borderline personality disorder (Angus and Gillies 1994).

Learning IPT

Research Training

Until recently, IPT was purely a research intervention. After publication of research successes, there has been increasing interest in learning the approach. Clinicians have been both curious to learn something that has been shown to work and pressured by managed care and other economic forces to deliver briefer therapies. Patients, too, reading about IPT in the lay and self-help presses, call IPT centers from across the United States seeking relief from depression.

In training for research studies, already experienced psychotherapists who are familiar with the treatment population (e.g., patients with major depression) first read the manual (Klerman et al. 1984), then often attend a training workshop, and finally begin supervised cases (Rounsaville et al. 1984; Weissman et al. 1982). Training cases are video- or audiotaped and reviewed with an established IPT supervisor on an hour-for-hour basis. Review of taped sessions reveals far more than process notes from sessions; moreover, research during IPT training found that process notes were not significantly correlated to session tapes (Chevron and Rounsaville 1983; Rounsaville et al. 1984).

Therapists generally have been asked to demonstrate competence in completing three training cases, with certification of competence based on review of tapes from these sessions by an IPT expert, before beginning research interventions. The number of cases is not entirely arbitrary; in our experience the trainee struggles to remember the mechanics of the therapy during the first case, may address different interpersonal problem areas in subsequent cases, and needs a while to develop comfort and facility with IPT techniques. At a certain point, usually after two or three cases, something seems to click, and both therapist and supervisor are won over.

Clinical Training

The reader who would like to use IPT need not necessarily undertake the rigors of research training. A simpler regimen would be to read the original Klerman et al. (1984) manual, possibly attend a course on IPT,[1] and then try doing IPT on one's own, or better still with peer supervision, referring to the manual for guidance.[2] Supervision also can be arranged. Although IPT can be combined with pharmacotherapy for depression, I encourage the reader to try using IPT alone with an appropriate patient. If you combine treatments, you may tend to attribute the patient's improvement to the medication rather than to this simple, potent psychotherapy. I also suggest that you begin with a patient who has major depression rather than dysthymic disorder. Because of their chronicity, dysthymic patients are probably more difficult to work with, and it helps to have the confidence of therapeutic success experiences under your belt to approach them with sustained assurance. I do encourage the reader to try IPT; it is hard to absorb confidence in an intervention simply from reading, but attempting to do the therapy is likely to both teach and convince you.

Supervision is the surest way to learn a treatment such as IPT. Based at Cornell

---

[1] We give courses on IPT once or twice a year at the Cornell Psychotherapy Institute in New York, as well as at the Annual Meeting of the American Psychiatric Association, and elsewhere.

[2] Other helpful background reading might include Klerman and Weissman 1993; Markowitz and Swartz, in press; and, for an annotated bibliography, Markowitz 1995a.

University Medical College in New York City, we have supervised people from as far away as Stockholm and The Hague, although this has involved some ingenuity and expense. Therapists have videotaped treatment sessions (in English), mailed the tape by overnight express, and arranged telephone supervision with an IPT expert who had viewed the tape. (My wife and colleague, Kathleen Clougherty, A.C.S.W., whom the late Gerald L. Klerman, M.D., trained, has been chief supervisor.) It also may be possible to arrange IPT supervision at other programs, such as the Western Psychiatric Institute and Clinic in Pittsburgh, PA; the University of Iowa; and York University and the University of Toronto in Ontario, Canada.

Early IPT research showed that experience and age distinguished good from weak IPT therapists; the former averaged more than 14 years and the latter averaged 7 years of clinical experience (Chevron et al. 1983). All were psychiatrists or clinical psychologists with psychodynamic backgrounds and respected clinical skills who had treated at least 10 depressed patients. Our impressionistic experience in training psychiatric residents, however, suggests that enthusiastic therapists with less experience can also learn IPT (Markowitz 1995b).

Psychodynamic Psychotherapists

For experienced psychodynamically trained therapists, the main shifts in focus are from past to present, from within-office transference to the patient's outside life focus, and from a focus on character to a medical model of psychiatric illness (see Table 3–3). It also means avoiding techniques such as interpretation of the transference. For therapists used to a long-term treatment model, adjusting to IPT requires greater activity, moving quickly to establish an explicit focus for treatment, using the time frame and structure of IPT to exert gentle pressure, and taking an involved, interactive, openly supportive role. Nonetheless, I should add that IPT does not seem to feel foreign to psychodynamically trained therapists. IPT is closest to psychodynamic therapy of the time-limited therapies designed to treat depressive disorders. A psychodynamic outlook can in many respects inform the IPT therapist about how to approach a patient who is dependent, paranoid, avoidant, etc. This psychodynamic reading of character is helpful so long as the focus remains on depression rather than character—again, in the setting of a mood disorder, what appears to be character may not be.

Time

The time limit and videotaping can take some time to get used to. Relax; in fact, 12 or 16 weeks turns out to be a long time. Think of time as an ally rather than a limita-

Table 3–3.   Shifting to an interpersonal psychotherapy (IPT) from a psychodynamic model

	Psychodynamic	IPT
Emphases	Transference	Real-life relationships
	fantasies	Feasible wishes
Time frame	Often past	"Here and now" present
Time limited	Often not	Yes
Structure	Free association	Interpersonal problem area
Psychopathologic model	Character	Medical model: depression
Goal	Understanding	Pragmatic success: solving problem area; euthymia

tion. The temporal limits of the treatment force both you and the patient into activity; patients are pushed to get better faster than they might otherwise consider possible. The therapist needs to be involved, to hew to the agreed upon focus, and to move the patient toward action in his or her life situation. At the same time, the therapist should not feel so hurried and pressured by the time frame as to sacrifice the therapeutic alliance or interrupt the patient's focus on affectively laden interpersonal experiences. It takes some experience to balance these opposing pulls.

Videotaping or Audiotaping

IPT sessions are taped for purposes of supervision and to monitor therapist adherence to study protocols. That is, taping ensures that therapists are delivering IPT rather than some other form of psychotherapy. Many psychotherapists who are not used to such monitoring feel uncomfortable with this at first but most quickly adjust. Reviewing videotapes is a highly educational, if sometimes humbling, experience.

1. Taping sessions requires the patient's informed written consent. You should have your patient fill out a consent form and sign it yourself. The patient is entitled to a copy of the consent form if he or she desires it.
2. Patients are often understandably concerned about committing their intimate feelings and thoughts to film, with the fear that their therapy might appear on nationwide TV some day. Your initial discussion of videotaping can reassure the patient on several counts.
   a. The form we use at Cornell University Medical College has separate "intramural" and "extramural" sections. You can have them sign only the former and use this to assure your patient that the tape will never leave the building.

b. It is important that the therapist state that he or she is as concerned as the patient about confidentiality, that the tapes will be kept under lock and key in the audiovisual department to ensure confidentiality, and that only researchers or supervisors associated with IPT will view the tapes.

c. The videotaping is in fact focused more on the therapist than on the patient: we are interested in the therapist's technique rather than the patient's history. Again, the film will be viewed only by therapists and supervisors to assess adherence to IPT technique.

d. Although the presence of the camera at first may be disruptive, experience confirms that after a short time both patient and therapist (the former more than the latter) tend to forget about it.

3. Like the patient, you too will adjust to being on camera. After some initial stiffness you may tend to forget that it is on or realize that it is recording terrific interactions. In general videotapes are a great teaching aid to supervision.

Other Time-Limited Therapies

Therapists versed in CBT or other time-limited psychotherapies need simply shift their emphasis (see Table 3–4). Cognitive therapy explores "hot" cognitions—irrational, "automatic" thoughts laden with affect—weighing the evidence for and against believing them to help the patient correct depressive distortions in his or her outlook. Cognitive therapists will find that IPT is less structured than CBT and that it focuses directly on affect and feelings rather than on approaching them through the conduit of automatic thoughts.

Psychiatric Residents[3]

With the future of long-term therapy, at least when conducted by psychiatrists, now threatened, residency education in psychotherapy is changing. Fewer programs provide instruction in psychodynamic therapy (Altshuler 1990) or even in psychotherapy generally (Rodenhauser 1992). Some of those that do continue teaching psychotherapy are shifting emphasis to include the proven, briefer treatments. This section describes my experience in teaching IPT and principles of short-term psychotherapy during the past 5 years in a time-limited therapy course at the Payne Whitney Clinic of New York Hospital, teaching IPT to 3rd postgraduate year (PGY-

---

[3] This section is based on Markowitz JC: "Teaching Interpersonal Psychotherapy to Psychiatric Residents." *Academic Psychiatry* 19:167–173, 1995. Used with permission.

Table 3–4.   Interpersonal psychotherapy (IPT) and cognitive-behavior therapy (CBT): commonalities and differences

Common factors

Nonspecific factors of psychotherapy

- Helping patient feel understood (relationship)
- Framework for understanding (rationale)
- Providing hope and optimism
- Psychoeducation
- Technique for getting better (ritual)
- (Novelty)

Common features of brief antidepressant psychotherapies

- Manualized
- Active
- Time-limited (with comparable time courses)
- Structured (CBT > IPT)
- "Here and now" current focus
- Can be combined with antidepressant medication
- Goals of self-assertion, mastery
- Ultimate goal of new skills for prophylaxis

Technical similarities

- Mobilizing patient to greater activity
- Linking mood to activities and (reactions to) events, albeit with different emphases
- Testing alternative solutions: "exploring options" versus "empirical hypothesis testing"/problem solving
- Addressing "expectations" versus "assumptions" about others
- Role playing

Differences

- IPT: medical model
- CBT: homework
- Focus on affect (IPT) versus thoughts (→ affect) (CBT)
- Differential therapeutics: which works better for whom in major depression?

  IPT: marital discord, cognitive dysfunction, ↑ symptom severity; CBT: interpersonal deficits, lack of interpersonal events

  Limited data; generally, both work

III) residents at Payne Whitney, and during 2 of those years also to PGY-III residents at the Columbia University College of Physicians and Surgeons.

Setting.   At Payne Whitney, I have helped to coordinate the PGY-III Brief Therapy course for the past 5 years, teaching its IPT segment and supervising residents in IPT. During part of this period, I also was invited to train faculty supervisors and teach PGY-III residents IPT at the Columbia residency program. Both residency programs have strong traditions of teaching long-term psychodynamic psychotherapy but less expertise in time-limited treatments. Both programs are revamping their brief therapy curricula to meet the future practice needs of today's trainees. At both sites IPT constitutes part of a broad exposure, over 6–12 months, to a range of time-limited psychotherapies that also includes CBT, behavioral therapy, brief focal psychodynamic psychotherapy, and other modalities. I had previously given workshops and courses on IPT in the United States and elsewhere that sometimes included residents but were attended mainly by more experienced psychotherapists.

Teaching IPT to residents.   IPT is not difficult to learn. Experienced clinicians, particularly if they have psychodynamic backgrounds, will find few technical innovations; IPT combines familiar interpersonal techniques into a coherent and intuitively appealing strategy that probably provides its treatment efficacy. But residents with a psychodynamic background do not come fully prepared.

Teaching IPT to residents presents problems and opportunities. My previous experience had been in retraining veteran clinicians to gain proficiency in IPT. Such therapists were often comfortable in developing a therapeutic alliance and could quickly "read" a patient's character and adjust accordingly. They were less comfortable at one aspect of brief therapy, which requires going out on a limb, putting oneself on the line. In my experience, therapists are more comfortable offering the promise of medication benefits to a depressed patient than offering themselves as antidepressant therapists. Particularly for accomplished psychodynamically trained clinicians, my emphases had been on taking the risk of greater activity in sessions, radiating greater therapeutic optimism, and avoiding non-IPT techniques.

PGY-III residents come to the brief therapy course with limited psychotherapeutic experience. They have done supportive work with severely ill inpatients but generally do not recognize this as psychotherapy, and they have begun one or two long-term psychodynamic cases in which they may tend toward an overly cautious, reticent, pseudoanalytic stance. In short, they lack clinical confidence; on the other hand, they have had little time to develop bad habits.

PGY-III residents are eager to learn and impressionable, yet they lack some of the psychotherapeutic reflexes and comfort with intimate patient contact that comes with experience. Hence asking them to take a newly active, confident role with patients can both exhilarate and frighten, even more than for veteran clinicians; they are often eager to try a proven treatment, but how can they confidently treat a morosely depressed patient when they lack the experience that provides the confidence? It is easier to take therapeutic chances when you are secure as a therapist. For residents, it is something of a blind leap of faith.

Among other things, IPT requires a therapist in training to

1. Manufacture therapeutic confidence (which may then solidify after seeing the results of a case or two)
2. Build a therapeutic alliance
3. Work quickly and actively without losing the affective connection with the patient
4. Conceptualize and deliver to the patient within the first few sessions an interpersonal formulation linking the patient's interpersonal situation to the onset of depression
5. Smoothly integrate other tasks (developing an interpersonal inventory of key relationships, giving the sick role) into ongoing dialogue with the patient, without seeming artificial or stilted
6. Maintain the therapeutic focus (Hall et al. 1990), even when the patient seeks to stray or an interesting, but irrelevant, topic arises
7. Present a reassuring, supportive, coherent, positive stance in contradiction to the depressed patient's negativism
8. (Hardest of all) terminate treatment even though both patient and therapist feel they make a wonderful team and that things are going swimmingly

These may be difficult tasks for an experienced psychotherapist to perform efficiently when learning IPT: for a relative psychotherapeutic novice, more so. Yet I have been impressed that residents' enthusiasm and flexibility compensate for lack of practice. Judging from videotaped sessions I have seen, they often show surprising finesse as well.

Teaching the particular techniques of IPT also provides the opportunity to elucidate general principles of brief therapy. For example, the leverage that a time limit provides; the importance of a coherent, focused approach to provide a framework for treatment; and questions of predicting specificity of response to treatments (Sotsky et al. 1991) and potential mechanisms of action. Teaching any one modality highlights similarities and contrasts with other psychotherapies.

Teaching format.   At each residency program I gave four initial weekly seminars, lasting 1½ hours apiece. Residents were urged to read the IPT manual (Klerman et al. 1984). This reading was supplemented with a handout that included a bibliography of IPT and brief therapy, a review of basic principles of brief therapy, comments on videotaping, and some tables of IPT strategies for easy reference as well as a reprint of a review article on IPT (Weissman and Markowitz 1994).

Seminars consisted mainly of lectures and open discussion. I encouraged interruptions for questions. Slides and videotapes, including a training videotape and excerpts from actual treatment sessions, complemented this discussion. Material covered included the history of interpersonal therapy, the research studies that validate its use, and comparisons with other therapies such as CBT; but the emphasis was on technique, for which the residents seemed avid. What is the appropriate stance to take with patients? How much do you let affect build before intervening? Is this maneuver interpersonal or cognitive? In the same way, I encourage residents to present IPT to a patient—there is a certain amount of parallel process here—I present IPT to them as a promising, exciting, interesting, hopeful therapy but also emphasize its limitations, the scope and differential therapeutics (Frances et al. 1984) of its prescription, and what we still do not understand (e.g., its active ingredients). Among its limitations: IPT has not been tested in the treatment of many disorders and has shown no benefit in treating opiate and cocaine abusers (Klerman and Weissman 1993).

Following the initial sessions, interspersed later in the year while the residents were learning other therapies, we held scheduled "booster sessions." These reinforced teaching points and allowed discussion, in a form of group supervision, of clinical experiences the residents had begun to have with IPT cases.

The response to the teaching sequence was quite positive. Yet learning a treatment technique requires more than listening; it requires practice. The key to providing the groundwork of solid training lies in moving the now motivated residents from the classroom to the office. This in turn requires adequate supervision. Supervisors of brief therapy should not in their hearts believe it to be a dilution or bastardization of "real," long-term or psychodynamic therapy. Rodenhauser's (1992) survey of the American Association of Directors of Psychiatric Residency Training noted the paucity of skill diversity and theoretical flexibility among factors limiting supervision. Yet for IPT, as mentioned, qualified supervisors are in relatively short supply; perhaps as a result, IPT is not mentioned among the types of residency psychotherapy experiences cited in that survey.

At Columbia, I spent a year supervising interested faculty members who then supervised residents the following year. At Payne Whitney, supervisors for the brief therapy program had been mainly psychoanalysts and psychodynamic psycho-therapists, only some of whom were truly comfortable with the principles of brief treatment and none of whom knew IPT. We substituted IPT-trained faculty available from our research programs to supervise resident IPT cases. The IPT manual provides guidelines for the therapy, but one learns clinical techniques by doing them. In research settings IPT has been taught by the skilled to the novice, a practice the Columbia program acknowledged and echoed in its plans by training supervisors a year ahead of its residents.

Videotaping is a worthwhile teaching and supervisory tool. It provides a record of sessions more accurate and less intrusive than process notes (Chevron and Roun-saville 1983). Videotaping allows the viewer the sometimes humbling recognition of gestures, phrases, and interactions that might be improved. Finally, tapes can be stopped to identify critical incidents in each session.

Even without much psychotherapeutic experience, residents arrived with prejudices. At Columbia in particular, where there appeared to have been a dichot-omy between psychopharmacologic and psychoanalytic approaches, the idea that a psychotherapy could be used to treat an axis I diagnosis like major depression re-quired some accommodation on the part of the residents. Some, imbued with a psy-choanalytic model, tended to regard this latecomer with skepticism. But residents responded well to the basic IPT theme connecting mood and environment, which made sense to them and to their patients. They liked the idea of a clear manual that spelled out general parameters of treatment and that manuals could be adapted to different treatment populations. They liked the medical model and the idea of differ-ential therapeutics: different, tested treatments tailored to different pathologies, rather than one Procrustean treatment for all patients. They asked sophisticated questions in class and in supervision. Discussing IPT as a distinct modality gave them a different, more complex perspective on other psychotherapies. And they gained self-confidence as therapists when they saw quick and sometimes dramatic results in their brief treatments.

Residents at both programs filled out course evaluations that were generally af-firmative but too sparse in number and content to yield meaningful analysis. My findings therefore rely on anecdote and impression. Despite their desultory return of evaluation forms, the residents encouraged me with their interest in the material, re-quests for supervision of cases, and questions about more advanced training. The Columbia faculty I trained reported a similar enthusiasm among their crop of resi-dent supervisees. IPT has made its mark through empirical demonstration of its effects, and it should have data on the efficacy of its teaching as well. For the moment I can offer less substance than I would wish.

Conclusion

Brevity, simplicity, and proven efficacy make IPT a candidate for reimbursement in future health care schemes, when brief therapies are likely to be the modal therapies for common disorders such as major depression. The same qualities may also make it clinically and heuristically attractive to residents, beyond any economic consequences. It differs from, but is not incompatible with, psychodynamic psychotherapy, which provides a solid foundation for the IPT approach, and its medical model allows combination of IPT and psychopharmacology without theoretical difficulty.

Although PGY-III residents must face the required level of activity in IPT without the security of broad experience and confidence in their role as therapist, they seem able to compensate with enthusiasm and vigor, to find aspects of the therapy appealing enough, and to be willing to go out on a limb and return bearing the ripe fruits of that experience. Both the residents and I were enthusiastic about the teaching experience, and the teaching often seemed to influence their subsequent work with patients. Videotaping of sessions is recommended, and qualified supervision is required, for a successful course.

This description is largely impressionistic, loosely based on comments derived from a few broadly positive resident evaluations. I have not attempted to address the role of brief therapy in psychotherapy curricula of residency training programs; my feeling, based more on my own training than anything else, is that IPT and other brief therapies, will take an increasingly important role in training but need not and should not supplant psychodynamic therapy as the metric for psychotherapy training. IPT might, however, be introduced earlier in training; PGY-II residents on inpatient services might benefit from at least an overview of therapies like IPT and CBT, which might give them tools for working with depressed inpatients (Miller et al. 1985, 1989; Thase et al. 1991). IPT can and should be taught to residents as well as to more advanced clinicians.

Summary

In this chapter, I have attempted to provide the reader with an overview of IPT and its techniques, access to some of its outcome research, and a description of training issues. If the reader now sees the utility of IPT for acute major depression, the next question is: How can it be adapted for the treatment of dysthymic patients?

Background Reading on
Interpersonal Psychotherapy

I have cited a number of references in the course of this chapter. The original manual and key reference is

Klerman GL, Weissman MM, Rounsaville BJ, et al: Interpersonal Psychotherapy of Depression. New York, Basic Books, 1984

A chapter on dysthymic disorder is one of several adaptations of IPT discussed in

Klerman GL, Weissman MM (eds): New Applications of Interpersonal Therapy. Washington, DC, American Psychiatric Press, 1993

A patient book, written for patients with major depression but also of probable utility to dysthymic patients, is

Weissman MM: Mastering Depression: A Patient's Guide to Interpersonal Psychotherapy. Albany, NY, Graywind Publications, 1995

This can be ordered through The Psychological Corporation, Order Service Center, P.O. Box 839954, San Antonio, TX 78283-3954; phone (800) 228-0752; fax (800) 232-1223.

The only self-help book that directly addresses dysthymic disorder is

Hirschfeld R: When the Blues Won't Go Away. New York, Macmillan, 1991

CHAPTER 4
Interpersonal Psychotherapy for Dysthymic Disorder

"If Winter comes, can Spring be far behind?"

—Shelley,
Ode to the West Wind

". . . Let us confidently hope that all will yet be well."

—Abraham Lincoln,
Farewell Address, Springfield, Illinois,
February 11, 1861

Difficulties in Adapting Interpersonal Psychotherapy to Dysthymic Disorder

Can a brief treatment treat a chronic disorder? It is one thing to pull a patient out of a relatively brief episode of illness, a more daunting prospect to tackle a lifelong condition. Not only is dysthymic disorder a more frightening condition for the therapist, it has specific disadvantages for interpersonal psychotherapy (IPT). Thus adapting IPT to treat dysthymic disorder poses at least four challenges.

For one thing, the clear dysjunction of recent life events from the temporal onset of the disorder seemingly vitiates the principal mechanism of IPT. IPT generally focuses on recent life changes linked to the onset of a mood disorder, yet dysthymic disorder begins in the distant past. *Dysthymic patients by definition lack an acute precipitant for their illness.* Thus although acute precipitants, such as a job crisis or a threatened divorce, may well bring a patient to treatment, even if the patient reports recent life events, what have they to do with the far-off beginning of the illness? How can the IPT therapist avoid an entanglement in the remote past and address the patient's current life problems while resolving this chronic disorder?

Another problem is. that dysthymic patients may be unable to remember any past period of euthymia. Most people recognize that their bad moods will not last indefinitely. Even patients who are experiencing an episode of recurrent major depression can helpfully be reminded that they have recovered from previous episodes and are likely to see better times again. Dysthymic patients, however, may lack the luxury of recalled euthymia. Having known only winter, they are understandably skeptical that spring will ever come.

Next, the deleterious effects of depression on social functioning—difficulty in self-assertion, expressing anger, taking social risks—tend to have become pervasive and ingrained over time in dysthymic patients. If the dysthymic episode has been lifelong, the patient may never have learned these social skills. Thus the treatment of dysthymic disorder involves not only the treatment of symptomatology, but the need to undo the chronic effects of the illness on personal and psychosocial functioning and to disentangle the effects of illness from personality and core identity. If one views the patient from the perspective of character or personality—which is precisely how the patient tends to view things—it is easy to see the therapist's task as almost impossible: to change a depressive character in a matter of weeks. (The reader will by now have recognized that this is not the perspective I prescribe.)

Finally, even if acute therapy can bring about the remission of a chronic disorder in 16 weeks, it seems unfair nevertheless to leave dangling a patient who has known only a few weeks of happiness. Patients who respond to acute IPT for dysthymic disorder (IPT-D) will therefore need to have stabilization in a maintenance treatment.

These are the issues that we faced in developing IPT as a treatment for dysthymic patients. In this development, we retained the basic core of IPT, the principles described in the last chapter, including the explicit case formulation, the medical model of depressive illness, the connection between current events and current mood, the focal interpersonal problem area, and the techniques of the intervention.

Adapting IPT to Dysthymic Disorder

Staying in the "Here and Now"

Case formulation is a key element of IPT (Markowitz and Swartz 1997). Unlike some psychotherapies, for which formulation may be important yet may reside largely in the therapist's mind, case formulation is a central, explicit element of IPT. Having gathered the history, the IPT therapist links the diagnosis of a mood disorder as a medical illness to the patient's current interpersonal problem area. This formulation provides an intuitively reasonable framework for treatment: namely

> How you are feeling has something to do with what's going on in your life.

Further, it provides a coherent focus for the treatment to follow:

> If you can understand and optimally solve your interpersonal problem area, you're bound to feel better.

Particularly for people who have had a recent life change, this makes a lot of sense and provides an optimistic alternative to the self-critical, hopeless outlook induced by the depressive illness. Agreement on this problem area opens the middle phase of IPT and invokes the particular strategies needed to deal with complicated bereavement, role dispute, role transition, or interpersonal deficits.

For dysthymic patients, the case formulation is equally crucial but handled differently. The dysthymic patient, too, needs an explanation to counter his or her deeply ingrained depressed ideas. Yet there is the temporal difficulty; even if recent events have upset the patient, the dysthymic illness has long predated them.

Moreover, whereas it is often relatively easy to reorient acutely depressed patients to an interpersonal explanation of their illness, dysthymic patients require some convincing. They have lived with their illness for so long! Indeed, they have lived with their depressive illness for so long that they have long ago accepted it as part of themselves, as (part of) their personality. Dysthymic disorder becomes chronically and stubbornly intertwined with the patient's self-concept.

The solution that we have developed is *to make IPT-D treatment itself an iatrogenic role transition.* Precisely because the patient is so convinced that he or she is personality disordered, temperamentally melancholic, the therapist relies on an interpersonal formulation to shake that self view.

> Your problem is that you *think* you're this way, but you've really been suffering from an illness all along, a treatable illness. Dysthymic disorder is a chronic form of depression that often responds to antidepressant medication, focused psychotherapy, or their combination.

The therapist should accordingly proceed with optimism while recognizing that the patient will not be easily convinced to rethink long-held beliefs. Acknowledging skepticism is part of the gambit of the formulation:

> You've been depressed for so long that you see this as part of your personality. It isn't: as we've just shown on the Hamilton Depression Rating Scale (Ham-D) (Hamilton 1960) and in the DSM-IV (American Psychiatric Association 1994), you have a medical illness called dysthymic disorder. You've had it (practically) all your life, so understandably you think that it's you. I don't expect you to believe me immediately, but I would like you to become an expert on dysthymic disorder and to consider the possibility that you've been suffering for a long time from a mood disorder. (It's as if you had polio all your life, and saw a limp as part of yourself, and then a cure came along.)
>
> What I'd like to do over the next 16 weeks is to help you to see what's the depression and what's you-when-you're-not-depressed. If I'm right—and you may gradually come to believe me—we can help you to see how dysthymic disorder interferes with your life and how you can change your life and your interactions with other people so that it doesn't have to interfere.

With this formulation the therapist introduces a role transition—a new view of one's life and life trajectory far more hopeful than most life events. It is a role transition, within therapy, from dysthymia to euthymia. This may seem artificial, at first, to the patient. Certainly the first time a therapist tries this, he or she may doubt the efficacy of such an intervention. But success breeds confidence, and I encourage the reader to try. Obviously if the formulation does not express confidence and optimism, the patient is less likely to be convinced.

If acute precipitants, even when present, are likely to prove less effective treatment as central interpersonal problem areas than they do in acute depressions, they may still provide opportunities for helping patients to explore new ways of handling interpersonal situations. We have found that any of the four IPT problem areas may affect dysthymic patients and have not seen the need to devise new interpersonal problem areas for dysthymic disorders. Yet their relative importance departs from acute depression.

When the therapist provides a formulation, linking the patient's mood disorder to an interpersonal problem area, it is often helpful to embellish it with a less generic, more personalized metaphor that uses the patient's own description of his or her life:

> So even though you feel that you're hiding your "black hole" from others, I think you're suffering from dysthymic disorder, a form of chronic depression, a chronic medical illness. I'd like to work with you for the next 16 weeks on a role transition into health, helping you to recognize that what has long felt like a "black hole" in your personality is a black illness called depression. You're not flawed, you're just ill. If you can learn to distinguish the illness of dysthymic disorder from the rest of your personality, and not let it control your life, you're very likely to feel better.

Grief, the first of the four IPT problem areas, is rarely the primary focus of IPT-D, albeit some patients do suffer from long complicated bereavements or experience exacerbation of preexisting dysthymic disorder. Role disputes may be less frequent for dysthymic patients because they are often not involved in intimate relationships. They still may have significant difficulties in work and social settings. Role transitions, interpersonal disputes, and interpersonal deficits allow more temporal latitude. Based on our previous experience in using IPT, the problem area of interpersonal deficits, the least developed and most difficult of the four, is probably best avoided when possible. Role transitions thus become the most useful IPT-D problem area. Each of the four problem areas is discussed in greater detail below.

Paucity of Euthymic Memories

Dysthymic patients may report having felt depressed "forever," "since the sperm hit the egg." For some this may be true: that they have had no more than hours, or at best days, of life without depression. Other patients, caught up in their mood, may selectively recall the dismal aspects of the past while forgetting brighter days.

Recall is an area of controversy (Bronisch and Klerman 1988; Prusoff et al. 1988) that bears upon this patient population. Studies have suggested that subjective recall of events is often unreliable beyond 6 months, particularly for depressed patients whose current outlook may retrospectively color memories of the past (Beck et al. 1979; Zimmerman et al. 1988). Angst and others (J. Angst, personal communication, 1993) found that some patients seemingly meeting criteria for DSM-III-R dysthymia, who described having been depressed much of their lives, were revealed by careful probing and prospective follow-up to suffer instead from brief recurrent depressions, spending the majority of their days euthymic, and thus not qualifying for dysthymia.

Such cognitive distortions may lead some patients who do meet diagnostic criteria for dysthymic disorder to report more continuously persistent symptoms and more impaired interpersonal functioning than they actually suffer. Accordingly, the IPT-D psychotherapist must be skeptical of blanket descriptions of dysfunction and seek areas and periods of higher functioning, genuine achievements that patients may have forgotten or discounted in their current dysphoric state, as evidence of potential for recuperation and growth. Detailed questioning is important to both the initial history and to subsequent weekly review of the patient's life situation, as it often brings to light positive nuances or events that the dysthymic patient has neglected.

Thus in taking a history of dysthymic patients, the therapist should probe for islands of euthymia, periods of higher functioning, and relative happiness that the patient may inadvertently have failed to recall. If found, these happier periods can help demonstrate to the patient a capacity for euthymia that the patient had discounted. Social strengths from those times—an ability to assert oneself, to achieve intimacy, to express anger—can be invoked to help the patient deal with a current life situation.

For many patients, however, particularly those with dysthymic disorder of insidious early onset, symptoms may indeed have been protracted and sustained. All the patient's energy may have been devoted to presenting a mask of quotidian mediocrity to hide the depression beneath while social skills and confidence never developed. For such patients the recognition of any areas of competence—often occupational, in areas of work that do not require social ease—may provide footholds to scale the sheer wall of self-esteem.

If the patient truly has no recollected experience of euthymia, the role of the therapist must be that of the first robin of spring, harbinger of a happier, richer, more optimistic future.

> You've been suffering from an illness that's held you back and that still makes
> it hard for you to see your nondepressed potential. If we work at this, the future
> can be much better than the dysthymic past.

Distinguishing Mood "State" From Personality "Trait"

A key difficulty in working with the dysthymic patient is the patient's sense that the depression is part of his or her personality. IPT-D turns this disadvantage to advantage by making this misconception the fulcrum of treatment, the focus of the iatrogenic role transition. (We have already seen in Chapter 2 that many patients who believe they have depressive personalities respond to pharmacotherapy or psychotherapy.) It is essential for both the patient and the therapist not to confuse "state" with "trait" (see pp. 10–12, pp. 21–22, and pp. 144–146).

IPT eschews claims to character change, acknowledging the limitations of any brief therapy in altering long-established character. The question remains, What is character? In treating dysthymic disorder, a major goal of IPT-D is to help the patient recognize which aspects of what he or she has considered inherent personality or temperament are in fact mood related and alterable. An important function of the treatment is to help the patient distinguish state from trait in a condition whose chronicity tends to merge the two.

An analogy may be made to pharmacotherapy of dysthymic disorder, in which patients responsive to antidepressants are newly cognizant of seeing the world, and themselves, from a novel perspective (Markowitz 1993). (This is, again, the *Listening to Prozac* phenomenon [Kramer 1993].) IPT-D does not propose to change character; but by treating a chronic affective illness that strongly influences identity and outlook, it may help the patient to reexamine long-standing behaviors and perceptions, to improve chronic difficulties in interpersonal functioning, and to improve pervasive poor self-image and self-esteem.

Maintenance Therapy

If IPT-D helps the patient as an acute treatment, ongoing psychotherapy appears clearly indicated to preserve treatment gains, allow the patient to consolidate newly acquired social skills, and prevent relapse.

CASE EXAMPLE

Ms. B, a 27-year-old, recently married college junior, presented for treatment because of worsening depression in the context of marital difficulties. She reported having felt depressed at least since the age of 12, when her parents had separated in a scandalous small-town divorce. Symptoms included depressed mood, fatigue, early morning awakening, poor appetite with mild weight loss, tension and irritability, an inner sense of helplessness, hopelessness, and intermittent thoughts of life not being worth living. Her initial Ham-D score was 15. She had previously failed two pharmacotherapy trials, in one instance because of inability to tolerate side effects. She had previously joined self-help groups and read many self-help books with slight gains but had not previously risked the intimacy of psychotherapy.

In IPT-D her marriage to a domineering, much older man who forbade her to work was examined in the context of a pattern of unsatisfactory previous relationships wherein she cared for cocaine addicts and other problematic partners. Her situation was formulated as a role dispute, and therapy focused on self-assertion in and renegotiation of her marital relationship. Unlike standard IPT, the therapy also stressed the role transition of recognizing that she was suffering from dysthymic disorder and of separating those feelings and behaviors influenced by chronic depression from her underlying personality.

As she learned to directly express—rather than intellectualize or shrug off—her anger, her symptoms waned, her confidence grew. She set better limits with her husband, won moral victories regarding her ability to work, and considered but decided against leaving a now improved marriage. After 16 weeks her Ham-D score had fallen to 8. Monthly booster sessions for 1 year, and bimonthly sessions in the second year, helped her to stabilize her new self-image and to maintain these gains for 2 years, with Ham-D scores ranging from 1 to 6.

Rationale for IPT-D

The underlying assumption is that dysthymic disorder of early onset is a mood disorder maintained by the malignant interaction of mood vulnerability and interpersonal deficits, each of which helps to perpetuate the other. Pharmacologic and psychological treatments, by affecting either arm of this balance, can effect remission. Combined treatment is likely to be still more effective by addressing both sides of the problem (see Figure 4–1).

Good therapies often work by "shaking up" the outlooks of demoralized patients. IPT-D attempts this

1. By giving the patient a new, simple, more hopeful formulation of his or her problem as a treatable illness rather than a personality type
2. By daring to use a brief, 16-week time frame with patients who have often endured open-ended and extremely lengthy psychotherapies
3. By the pressure that the time limit places on both patient and therapist to work rapidly and effectively

Again, the chronicity of dysthymic disorder may daunt many psychotherapists into setting modest goals and settling in for a lengthy treatment. The brevity of IPT-D instills an urgency that helps shake patients from their inertia and forestalls therapists' collusion with patients' despair. Thus length of the intervention is main-

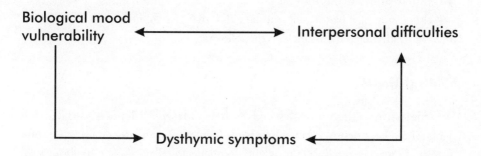

Figure 4–1.

tained at the standard 16–18 sessions used for major depression, in a dosage of once or twice weekly 50-minute sessions during the first 2 weeks and weekly sessions thereafter. The option to double sessions in the first 2 weeks allows exploration of the patient's lengthy history and building of the treatment alliance. Chronicity of dysthymic maladaptive behaviors might be supposed to need longer to change them, but our pilot data (Chapter 2) contradict this. The active therapeutic stance avoids long silences and thereby cuts depressive rumination.

Interpersonal therapists must not be afraid to focus the therapy for the patient, to indicate that certain areas are more important than others—given the time frame and the goal of treating depression—to actively provide encouragement and explore options, and to offer direct suggestions when appropriate. I have been impressed that this active, brief approach works even for a chronic condition such as dysthymic disorder. Moreover, patients soon catch on. After a few sessions they know what is required of them and often need little guidance in addressing interpersonal issues.

Interpersonal therapy makes no presumptions about causality but builds on the clinical and epidemiologic evidence that depression occurs in an interpersonal context and that addressing current interpersonal problems contributes to recovery. The goal of IPT-D is to assist the patient in coping with the chronic interpersonal perturbations of dysthymic disorder as a strategy for treating both depressive symptoms and interpersonal functioning.

The prime difference between patients with dysthymic disorder and those with acute depression is precisely the chronicity of their illness. Over time, depression tends to pervade personality; dysthymic disorder has erosive and enduring effects in compromising cognitive and interpersonal functioning. IPT addresses the social and interpersonal difficulties that dysthymic patients face, providing a rationale for using IPT-D to treat dysthymic disorder.

Other, standard features of standard IPT that remain important to the treatment of dysthymic patients include the following.

Medical Model

Defining dysthymic disorder as a mood disorder and medical illness is crucial for patients whose long-depressed existence leads them to consider depressive symptoms as part of their personality. This redefinition helps to relieve them of guilt for their condition and encourages them to see symptoms as ego-dystonic rather than aspects of their core selves. Unlike a psychodynamic approach, IPT never suggests that patients might "want" to be depressed for conflictual reasons but rather that they have an illness that, once recognized, they can treat and recover from.

In diagnosing dysthymic disorder, the IPT-D therapist pulls out DSM-IV and the Ham-D as proof, forcing the patient into a therapeutic "role transition" beginning in the treatment itself. In IPT-D the patient then learns to recognize symptoms as ego-dystonic rather than part of self. This is a role transition into health and out of an illness that has previously been perceived as part of the individual's personality.

This redefinition has several advantages:

1. It changes the usual IPT approach from addressing a reaction to negative acute stressors (e.g., complicated bereavement) into the provision (by the therapist) of a positive stressor: one that simultaneously psychoeducates the patient about his or her illness, offers a treatment option where none may have been apparent, and precipitates a role transition that will begin in treatment and continue thereafter.
2. It helps the patient begin to separate symptoms from latent character and to make those symptoms ego-dystonic.
3. It limits the tendency of both therapist and patient to see chronic symptoms and interpersonal patterns as inherently ingrained and hopeless, because they may well lift with the mood disorder. Dysthymic character features may reflect a chronic state rather than a true trait.

What Does the Patient Want? An Exploration of Options

Depressed patients all too often feel that they do not deserve fulfillment, that their goals are unattainable, or that they have no options. An important aspect of IPT is to explore what the patient wants and what options he or she has to achieve those goals. This takes on new urgency for a dysthymic patient who may long before have become resigned to an unhappy life situation. The recognition that options do exist and can be pursued can be extraordinarily empowering for such patients.

"Here-and-Now" Focus

Although the patient may have been depressed since childhood, the therapist focuses treatment on current life relationships and situations. The emphasis may be on how the patient can address these differently than in the past, given recognition of dysthymic disorder. As the patient improves, however, the "here and now" may take on a new dimension. Patients who have lived lives according to depressed assumptions may now need to construct a "new track record" for themselves, a new history and sense of self beginning with the onset of euthymia. In light of the euthymic present they may be able to gain perspective on their dysthymic past.

Socialization and Activity

Socialization and activity are again important for two reasons. Activity in itself has some antidepressant benefit. Although a natural tendency of depressed patients is to isolate themselves, it can also be the worst thing they can do. Isolation provides plenty of time for rumination, sitting home alone and thinking about how little one is doing. Social interactions also have particular importance to the IPT process. The focus of treatment is not so much on what goes on in the therapist's office as what occurs during the patient's week. Even negative interactions are better than none, because therapist and patient can then analyze what went wrong. If the patient has not had any social contacts, there is little to discuss in sessions.

Optimism

The influence of a positive outlook in countering the negative view of depressed patients cannot be overstated. Our experience with pilot dysthymic patients and with another group of seemingly "hopeless," HIV-positive depressed patients indicates that a confident therapist with a coherent treatment strategy can help a patient make dramatic changes in a short time. Expression of therapeutic optimism is particularly important to buoy the patient during the inevitable weeks when change may not seem to be occurring:

> It's a process. It takes time to change . . . though not too much time.

If interactions the patient attempts do not go well, or less well than planned, they are optimistically viewed as opportunities for learning, for developing new options and strategies. The therapist's primary emphasis is that the patient is making efforts to change his or her life and mood disorder and that sooner or later they are likely to succeed; the possibility of recovery of dysthymic disorder remains undimmed.

Structure of Treatment

Length of the intervention is the standard range of 16–18 sessions used for acute major depression. It may consist either of 16 weekly sessions or of a dosage of twice-weekly 50-minute sessions during the first 2 weeks and weekly sessions thereafter. This increased early frequency speeds the taking of what may be a protracted history and cements a treatment alliance. Beyond this, therapy sessions should not be too frequent; weekly spacing allows the patient time between sessions to try out new interpersonal maneuvers. More frequent sessions might simply increase dependency on the therapist. Because dysthymic subjects have lived longer with their maladaptive behaviors, it might be supposed they would need longer to change them, but our pilot data contradict this.

The structure of the IPT phases—early, middle, and late—remains unchanged. Subjects completing acute treatment are offered booster sessions of varying frequency, but at least monthly for 6 months (cf. Frank et al. 1990), to help maintain and consolidate their acute gains.

Initial Sessions

The first one to three sessions of IPT-D encompass multiple goals, most of which involve diagnosing the patient, setting a framework for the treatment to follow and beginning to provide therapeutic relief (see Table 4–1 and Chapter 3). The goals include establishing the diagnosis of dysthymic disorder; collecting data, including careful medical and medication histories and an interpersonal inventory; explaining the nature of both the mood disorder and the patient role; establishing interpersonal problem areas and linking them to diagnosis in a treatment contract; pursuing a treatment alliance, providing psychoeducation about dysthymic disorder, and imparting hope.

Table 4–1. Outline of IPT-D therapist's tasks and techniques: initial sessions

A. Dealing with dysthymic disorder
   1. Review depressive symptoms
   2. Give the syndrome a name: dysthymic disorder
   3. Explain dysthymic disorder and the treatment
   4. Give the patient the "sick role"
B. Relate dysthymic disorder to interpersonal context

Review current and past interpersonal relationships as they relate to current depressive symptoms. Determine with the patient the interpersonal inventory:
   1. Nature of interaction with significant persons
   2. Expectations of patient and significant persons from one another, and whether these were fulfilled
   3. Satisfying and unsatisfying aspects of the relationships
   4. Changes the patient wants in the relationships
C. Identify the major problem area
   1. Determine problem areas related to currently sustaining depressive symptoms and set treatment goals
   2. Determine which relationships or aspects of relationships are related to the depression and what might change in it
   3. Identify the iatrogenic role transition of IPT-D
D. Explain the IPT concepts and contract
   1. Outline your understanding of the problem, linking problem area to dysthymic disorder (interpersonal formulation)
   2. Agree on treatment goals
   3. Describe procedures of IPT: "here and now" focus, need for patient to discuss important concerns; review of current interpersonal relations; discussion of practical aspects of treatment—length, frequency, times, policy for missed appointments
E. Instill hope
F. Psychoeducation about dysthymic disorder

Establishing the Diagnosis

Patients may not recognize depression as such, unthinkingly accepting their mood, neurovegetative symptoms, and hopelessness as part of their core sense of identity. In fact, dysthymic patients have been depressed for so long that they typically cannot distinguish their mood disorder from their character. The exposition of the therapeutic drama consists of carefully diagnosing the patient's disorder and then presenting it to him or her as a discrete, treatable disorder. The Ham-D and Cornell Dysthymia Rating Scale (Mason and Kocsis 1989; Mason et al. 1993b) provide symptomatic guidelines. In our treatment studies, even though the patient will have met criteria for dysthymic disorder on a structured clinical interview such as the Structured Clinical Interview for DSM (Spitzer and Williams 1985) to enter treatment, diagnosis by the therapist is an important gambit in IPT.

Psychiatric evaluation includes a history of current illness, history of previous psychopathology and psychiatric treatment, family history of psychiatric disorders, and mental status examination. Particular attention is paid to the quality, duration, expectations, and outcome of the patient's past and present relationships, the interpersonal inventory.

Diagnosis follows DSM-IV criteria.

Taking the Interpersonal Inventory

The interpersonal inventory is a catalogue of the patient's important relationships, beginning with childhood but focusing on the recent past and present. The therapist should explore patterns of interpersonal behavior, including expectations of others, especially nonreciprocal expectations, the nature of interactions, and the patient's perceived role in life. This includes sexual history and relationships with parents, siblings, lovers, confidants, friends, and co-workers. The history and state of current relationships, and recent changes in them, deserve detailed attention. Are there people the patient can confide in and rely on for support? Has the patient been able to mourn losses? Both areas of difficulty and interpersonal assets should be noted.

History of previous psychiatric treatments also requires careful inquiry. Which psychotherapeutic and psychopharmacologic treatments has the patient received? What issues were discussed, what were the patient's expectations, and does he or she feel that the therapy was beneficial? What does the patient want from therapy now? Pointing out instances of inadequate pharmacologic doses and that psychotherapies have been "generic" rather than targeted at depression or dysthymic disorder per se may help patients feel less like failures and enhance their expectations of the IPT-D trial. (Nonpsychiatric psychotherapists might suggest consultation with a psychopharmacologist at this point to explore the adequacy of prior, and the prospects for future, antidepressant medication trials.) Lack of response to past appropriate treatments should be acknowledged without concession of hopelessness. Because of the chronicity of the syndrome, and because most dysthymic individuals seeking treatment will have already undergone one or more unsuccessful therapies (Kocsis et al. 1986; Markowitz et al. 1992a), the psychiatric history may be lengthy.

The therapist also should determine how the patient has spent his or her *leisure time* in the past and how that may have changed. A key question is what the patient wants from relationships and whether these goals may be realistically achieved. Birthdays, anniversaries, and important holidays—and how the patient deals with them—are noteworthy for their interpersonal impact during the course of treatment.

For dysthymic individuals, the work setting often provides the major social contacts; there they often attempt simply to maintain a facade of normalcy, to not let their depression show. Many lack active sexual and emotionally intimate relationships and minimize those friendships they do have. Dysthymic patients often have difficulty ending even unsatisfactory relationships, preferring miserable company to loneliness and fearing "I won't be able to meet anyone . . . there's no one out there who could care about me." Relationships with ex-lovers, which the patient may minimize in his or her initial descriptions, should be carefully examined to see whether they still provide some emotional sustenance.

Establishing the Problem Area

Most of the dysthymic patients we have treated have had some interpersonal difficulties or apparent deficits. These often appeared related to their depressed mood: extreme fear of rejection, leading to the avoidance of relationships; or fear of abandonment, with a subsequent willingness to accept inequities in those relationships they do have. Interpersonal deficits have been the least theoretically developed IPT problem area of IPT, and patients with such deficits present the greatest challenge to treatment. Hence we have found it preferable to choose alternative foci when they exist, working on interpersonal deficits within the context of grief, interpersonal dispute, or especially role transition.

Indeed, we suspect that many patients who have been deemed to have interpersonal deficits have in fact suffered from dysthymic disorder. For such patients and their therapists, the iatrogenic role transition may provide a much more hopeful framework and formulation than the interpersonal deficits model. Again, a mood disorder appears far more easily treatable than does a character flaw.

Patient and therapist should decide on the problem area, or two at most, that best fits the patient's situation and address the interpersonal difficulties he or she would most like to change. The idea of IPT-D itself as an iatrogenic role transition can be used as an overarching framework in which to consider current life perturbations such as grief, role disputes, and other role transitions.

The patient's input is a necessary factor in this determination.

Research on IPT has not previously considered the reliability with which therapists choose problem areas. This manual contains the Interpersonal Problem Area
Rating Scale (IPARS; Appendix 3), which we use at Cornell to assess this. The IPARS
may be useful for beginning IPT therapists as a checklist to ensure that they have
considered all possible areas of interpersonal focus.

The IPT Outcome Scale, also in Appendix 3, may be useful for measuring the effect of the treatment on the interpersonal problem area that has been the focus of the
treatment.

The Sick Role

An important aspect of initiating therapy is legitimizing the patient's role. The patient is given the "sick role" defined by Parsons (1951); this exempts him or her from
certain ordinary social obligations and pressures, defines him or her as needing help,
and requires his or her cooperation in recovering from the disease state as quickly as
possible. Defining the patient as suffering from a discrete psychiatric disorder allows
him or her to distinguish symptoms as ego-dystonic rather than a defective attribute
of him- or herself—a crucial if difficult differentiation for the lifelong dysthymic individual. Recognition that he or she has an illness can help to render symptoms ego-
dystonic rather than accepted, limiting self-blame for "laziness" and other depressive symptoms. The sick role validates patient's needs to decrease work and social
pressures while increasing particular interpersonal contacts and activities.

Coyne (1976) and others have demonstrated that, although depression initially
may evoke sympathy and support, it subsequently yields impatience, frustration,
and withdrawal by those in the environment, who come to see the symptoms as will-
fully unpleasant. Those around the patient may become critical, even hostile, and
may withdraw from what they see as morally weak behavior (Klerman et al. 1984,
pp. 61–66). High levels of expressed emotion in a marriage, marital distress, and
patients' perceptions of criticism by spouses all have been associated with depressive
relapse (Hooley and Teasdale 1989). To extend the understanding of the sick role to
the patient's family, with the aim of reducing interpersonal pressures and levels of
expressed emotion, the patient may be given educational material or brochures explaining depression in an interpersonal context (Markowitz and Kocsis 1995; Weissman 1995).

At the same time that assuming the sick role may relieve self-criticism and social
pressures on the patient, it should not provide an excuse for regressive social withdrawal. Interpersonal contact is crucial to providing material for IPT and for changing the behaviors, such as social withdrawal, that characterize dysthymic disorder.

The ultimate resolution of the sick role is a graduation into what for dysthymic individuals may be a novel healthy role.

Even more than the standard medical model used in IPT for acute depression, IPT-D stresses the diagnosis of dysthymic disorder as an often previously unrecognized disorder the patient has, precipitating a "role transition" simply in bestowing the sick role. Having this role transition obviates the use of an interpersonal deficit model. The role transition is easier to address and appears more appropriate in working with dysthymic patients than a deficit model that may in fact be confusing chronic mood state with trait.

Developing the Treatment Plan

The patient may or may not have had previous experience in psychotherapy and needs to understand the patient's role in IPT. This includes choosing topics and offering material for sessions, with an emphasis on thoughts and feelings about recent interpersonal life events.

The therapist should explain that the test of therapy is what the patient accomplishes between sessions in "real life"; the therapy is used to develop strategies for the patient's life outside the office. Patients who have previously been in dynamic or cognitive psychotherapy may need help in understanding differences in the IPT patient role. IPT does not focus on dreams or the patient's early development, as in psychodynamic therapies. (If a patient brings in a dream, you may be able to draw on interpersonal themes in the manifest content but should refocus the session on the patient's current waking situation.)

Nor does the IPT therapist assign formal homework, as in cognitive-behavioral therapy. On the other hand, a form of homework is implicit in IPT, inasmuch as the therapy presses the patient to make changes in the interpersonal life situation on which the treatment is focused. And if, for example, the patient is ambivalently holding back in a treatment focusing on confronting a spouse's behavior in a role dispute, the therapist might suggest,

> Why not try to have the conversation with your husband that we talked about today? Let him know how you're feeling about that.

The Formulation

Once convinced of the diagnosis of dysthymic disorder, the therapist presents the constellation of somatic, cognitive, and emotional symptoms as a recognizable and treatable diagnosis. It may be helpful to show the patient the DSM-IV as evidence that the symptoms he or she has long taken for granted are in fact a disorder. The therapist lists the elicited signs and symptoms of dysthymic disorder, indicates that they confirm the diagnosis, and then relates them to the crucial problem area(s).

These symptoms are part of chronic depression, or dysthymic disorder, which is a treatable medical illness. That depression is related to what has been happening in [the specific interpersonal situation]. Because you've been depressed for so long—perhaps all your life—it may be hard to recognize that you have a disorder, that this isn't part of you, part of your personality.

Although your situation feels hopeless, and untreatable, it isn't: that feeling is a paradoxical symptom of a highly treatable and common disorder. More than 8% of the U.S. population develops a significant depression in their lifetime, and more than 3% have the kind of long-lasting depression you do. Depression nearly always improves with treatment. Depression affects and is affected by interpersonal relationships [it is helpful here to point out social withdrawal, losses, and interpersonal difficulties in the patient's own case] and interpersonal therapy, a brief treatment based on this connection, has been shown in research studies to be highly effective in treating depression. We'll try to understand what current stresses and relationships in your life may be contributing to depression and how your depressed feelings affect how you behave in relationships.

Moreover, this therapy is going to function as *a role transition out of dysthymic disorder and into healthier functioning.* As we examine your interactions with your social environment, I'm going to be encouraging you to recognize how the depressive illness of dysthymic disorder interferes with your life. We'll explore other options that will help you both handle situations better and feel better.

Obtaining the Patient's Agreement to the Formulation

In addition to explaining the diagnosis of dysthymic disorder, the therapist should weave into his or her recapitulation of the patient's story the interpersonal events relevant to the problem areas on which he or she proposes therapy should focus. Therapist and patient should explicitly agree on an interpersonal focus in one or two of the problem areas as the target for the treatment to follow (i.e., grief, role dispute, role transition). *(Note:* At the end of the first session, and again later if need be after having decided on the interpersonal formulation and problem area[s], the therapist should fill out the IPARS [see Appendix 3].)

Establishing a Therapeutic Alliance

The Epidemiologic Catchment Area study established that dysthymic individuals are frequent users of health and mental health services (Weissman et al. 1988). It is consequently important to explore previous interpersonal relationships with therapists and other caretakers, including expectations, the nature of treatment, and its outcome. Dysthymic patients who have already had courses of psychotherapy or pharmacotherapy may describe hopelessness about the outcome of the current treatment based on unrealistic assessments of past treatment. The IPT therapist can offer confident answers about the treatment and outcome of depression.

As IPT therapists gather information about a patient's life and form hypotheses about interpersonal associations with depression, they should teach the patient his or her role while fostering a supportive, encouraging alliance. Therapists should underscore the nature and limits of the therapeutic relationship and a sense of a mutual endeavor (albeit with the focus squarely on the patient). Psychoeducation and the instilling of hope are further aspects of initiating treatment that can help to build trust.

Because dysthymic patients generally need to rethink their whole approach to relationships, the therapeutic relationship takes on greater importance than in IPT for acute depression. It provides important interpersonal modeling, particularly for subjects with interpersonal deficits. Examples include the following tendencies of the subject:

- To apologize to the therapist
- To present him- or herself as superficially "normal," fearing to reveal a "defective" self
- To avoid the dual risks of expressing anger and of angering the therapist

The therapist should delve for and encourage the expression of dissatisfaction about the therapist and therapy, gently confronting and exploring the patient's tendency to idealize and empower the therapist while presenting him- or herself as helpless, ineffectual, and apologetic. This attention to the therapy should not, however, distract from the primary focus on the patient's interpersonal functioning outside the office.

The treatment should be framed as a collaboration, moreover, as a joint venture in which the patient's wishes, desires, and goals are paramount. Addressing interpersonal issues in the therapeutic relationship not only strengthens the working alliance but also can provide a springboard for parallel issues in other interpersonal situations.

One patient was markedly deferential in sessions, apologizing for imagined missteps and seeming to await the therapist's lead. Identifying this in treatment revealed it to be a general tendency in her relationships. Understanding this apologetic behavior as a consequence of her dysthymic disorder, she was able to modify it both in sessions and elsewhere.

The stance of the IPT therapist is as an empathic expert who is confident, supportive, and helpful. The transference is not generally addressed or manipulated in IPT. For example, if a patient arrived late for several sessions, the therapist would generally focus on the limited time available for work rather than trying to examine the patient's relationship with the therapist.

I know it's hard to get to sessions when you don't have much energy and feel so discouraged. Do the best you can, though, because we unfortunately we only have nine sessions left, and it's important that we make the most of the time we have to help you get better.

Psychoeducation

This should include the nature of depression, symptoms of dysthymic disorder, and the likely course and effectiveness of its treatment. A matter-of-fact and confident tone, backed by reference to appropriate research studies, can help the patient feel that there is a way to structure and deal with his or her experience.

When you've been depressed for years, as you have been, it's hard to recognize that you have an illness, to see that the disorder isn't you. These symptoms—sleep disturbance, pessimism, fatigue, not wanting to be around people, wishing you were dead—are as much symptoms of depression as your feeling blue is. And you can get control over them instead of having them control you.

I'm going to keep reminding you of this, because I want you to understand what's illness, not you, and that it doesn't have to continue to be that way. As we work on the interpersonal factors that are part of dysthymic disorder, the symptoms will start to go away.

Appendixes 1 and 2 contain information sheets about dysthymic disorder that may be helpful for patients and their families. Self-help books on IPT (Weissman 1995) and on dysthymic disorder (Hirschfeld 1991) also may serve the cause of psychoeducation.

Instilling Hope

This is to some degree an extension of psychoeducation, but it cannot be overemphasized. From the start, the IPT therapist should impart hope. Depression is a treatable illness, IPT an effective treatment; there always are options, even if hard to see when depressed.

> You're suffering a lot from [symptoms], but those are symptoms of depression; as treatment proceeds you should begin to feel better. . . . You have options in life that dysthymic disorder has undoubtedly kept you from fully exploring. It's harder to do everything when you're depressed—particularly when you don't even realize that you are depressed, when you think that the problem is you rather than dysthymic disorder. You've been fighting all your life with one hand tied behind your back.

Middle Sessions

Initiating the Middle Sessions

The middle phase of therapy (approximately sessions 3–12) begins with creation of and agreement on a treatment contract. This stage of IPT-D has two goals: 1) the alleviation of depressive symptoms and 2) assisting the patient to explore and rethink the interpersonal problems on which the treatment centers.

The therapist should begin sessions with the statement,

> Tell me how you have been since we last met. [Or, e.g., if the focus is an interpersonal dispute: How have you been doing with your lover since we last met?]

This maintains the focus on current interpersonal issues. It emphasizes that the therapist will take an active, interested role and maintain thematic continuity from session to session. In contrast, a dynamic therapist might say nothing or ask about thoughts and feelings, a cognitive therapist would arrange an agenda and query depressive cognitions, and a supportive therapist might simply ask how the patient is feeling.

As noted in Chapter 3, patients usually respond to the opening in one of two ways, either reporting depressive symptoms or interpersonal events. If the patient describes depressive symptoms, the therapist can seek to relate these to contemporary interpersonal events and the appropriate problem area. The symptoms deserve careful attention: they should be elicited in detail, and, in psychoeducational mode, labeled as symptoms of a chronic depressive disorder. The patient can then be reassured that he or she is amenable to treatment:

> Yes, having no energy and difficulty concentrating are symptoms of your dysthymic disorder; so is the lack of sleep. Those symptoms certainly can interfere [at the office/with your relationship]. They'll improve as the treatment begins to take effect.

A bridging statement then connects this to an interpersonal framework. Where a cognitive therapist might address automatic thoughts connected with the work situation, the IPT intervention might be

> Your symptoms seem to fluctuate depending upon how you're getting along with [your boss/your lover].

If the patient offers an interpersonal issue, the therapist should listen, explore the material, and eventually tie the theme to symptomatic fluctuation. Fidelity to the IPT problem area has been an important predictor of therapeutic outcome (Frank et al. 1991a).

Applicability of the Four Problem Areas

The sections that follow modify the application of the four IPT problem areas (Klerman et al. 1984) to the treatment of dysthymic patients based on clinical experience and pilot research to date. Work revolves around one or two problem areas that have been identified. Our discussion relies not only on the 17 pilot cases reported above but on ongoing experience with dysthymic patients in several forms of psychotherapy, including IPT-D and combined psychopharmacotherapy.

The "here-and-now" framework of IPT helps maintain a helpful focus, avoiding depressive ruminations on the "there and then," including past failures and losses. It mobilizes internal resources by encouraging a sense of mastery of the situation and external supports by facilitating interpersonal relationships.

Number of problem areas.   Many patients will qualify for more than one interpersonal problem area. Limiting the number of problem areas to one or at most two is important in honing the focus of the treatment. Choose too many, and little may get done. Given a choice, role transition is useful as a broad umbrella that can encompass various life changes.

Problem areas sometimes emerge in the course of therapy: for example, a patient working on a role transition revealed late in the course of treatment a long-standing covert dispute between himself and his lover in what he had previously declared an unproblematic relationship. Therapists should search critically for latent or masked problem areas and then should concentrate the therapy on one or at most two problem areas.

Ending sessions.   The therapist should end sessions by briefly summarizing key themes or new understandings that have emerged in the preceding three quarters of an hour.

> So one thing that's clearer today is how you've avoided arguing with your husband for fear he'd leave you . . . .

This is an opportunity to solidify gains and to assess the patient's response to these therapeutic developments. Sessions should end on time and address business such as arranging the next appointment, explaining vacation coverage, etc.

Grief

Depression has long been associated with object loss. For the purposes of IPT, grief is defined as the death of a loved one in a spousal or sexual relationship, one's biological family, or one's circle of friends. Other losses, such as divorce, illness, the loss of a job, etc., should be considered role transitions.

Uncomplicated grief is not considered a mental disorder (American Psychiatric Association 1994); most mourners do not require professional help, particularly if bolstered by interpersonal supports (Lindemann 1944). Because of the chronicity of dysthymic symptoms, acute grief is rarely a focus of IPT-D. Nonetheless, when the death of a significant other exacerbates dysthymic disorder, it provides an excellent focus for exploration of the exquisite sensitivity to loss shown by dysthymic patients and their difficulty in expressing sadness, anger, and other ambivalently held feelings.

Treating complicated bereavement requires facilitating the process of mourning (see Table 4–2). Depressive symptoms are reviewed, their onset is related to the death of significant others, and the relationship between the patient and the deceased is reconstructed. The patient's experience of events leading up to the death, his or her response to the death itself, and his or her subsequent attempts to grieve bear careful examination. Unmet expectations, things the patient would like to have

---

Table 4–2.   Outline of IPT-D goals and techniques: intermediate sessions—grief

---

A. Goals

    1. Facilitate the mourning process

    2. Help the patient reestablish interest and relationships to substitute for what has been lost

B. Strategies

    1. Review depressive symptoms

    2. Relate symptom onset or exacerbation to death of significant other

    3. Reconstruct the patient's relationship with the deceased

    4. Describe the sequence and consequences of events just prior to, during, and after the death

    5. Explore associated feelings (negative and positive)

    6. Consider possible ways of becoming involved with others

---

said, and positive and negative feelings about the lost other are aired. To facilitate catharsis, the therapist often encourages the patient to visit the grave, to look at (or bring in to sessions) photographs of the deceased, to clean out a room that has been preserved as a shrine, or to discuss the loss with others. As grieving proceeds in and out of the IPT sessions, the patient can gradually be encouraged to explore new, compensatory relationships.

> Mr. C, a 46-year-old, never-married, white Jewish photographer, had never mourned the nearly simultaneous deaths of his father and only brother 20 years before. Although there were suggestions of depression preceding these twin events, his dysthymic disorder had significantly worsened thereafter. His business was only marginally successful. He felt tormented and humiliated by his dealings with female relatives and was ambivalently involved with a girlfriend whose attempts at intimacy frightened him.
>
> Therapist and patient agreed on the two problem areas of complicated bereavement (grief) as well as an intratherapy role transition out of dysthymic disorder. Grieving was recognized as an important step toward better functioning. The patient decided to visit the graves of his dead male relatives, where he "boo-hooed" and subsequently felt better. He also reviewed family photograph albums. In therapy sessions he discussed his sense of guilt as the lone surviving man in the family. He took some steps to improve his career, put his house in order, and found new options for dealing with women. His life, which patient and therapist noted seemed to have come to a standstill after the deaths, gathered new momentum and his mood improved.

Depressed individuals tend to idealize the lost person and the time before the loss and to demonize themselves and the present. One important aspect of complicated bereavement is to build a more balanced, three-dimensional view of the lost other and of the patient. It is also important to place mourning in the larger context of pre-existing dysthymic disorder and to relate the current death to previous losses where applicable.

Interpersonal Role Dispute

Dysthymic disorder tends to produce unequal relationships of limited intimacy. Dysthymic patients tend to social isolation, which may be absolute or limit their relationships to superficiality. When dysthymic individuals succeed in appearing "normal" to others who encounter them, it is usually at the cost of great internal tension because they inwardly feel inferior, bad, not worth knowing. Less likely to have intimate relationships, they are also likely to understate the value of those relationships they do have. When they do marry or otherwise risk intimacy, their relationships tend to be masochistic. Feeling unworthy of better, they may cling to dysfunctional relationships and roles for fear of losing the little they have.

In examining an existing relationship, the IPT therapist and patient should consider what each partner wants and expects from it, whether disputes exist or have reached an impasse, and, if so, what options are available to the patient to alter the relationship (see Table 4–3). Is the relationship genuinely satisfying, or is the patient settling for an unsatisfactory situation because of feelings of inadequacy? Patients may require some prodding to explore what they really desire from relationships, as opposed to what they have been accustomed to receiving or thinking they deserve. What they themselves want is a concept often not considered by patients who have predicated their relationships and lives on caretaking, fulfilling the wishes of others as a way of excusing their self-perceived leprosy (i.e., "self-defeating").

> Your depressed mood has affected your views about the relationship with
> _____. Are things really the way you want them to be?

Once the patient's needs and desires are uncovered, he or she can explore the options available.

Anger.   A characteristic problem of dysthymic individuals involved in relationships is suppression of anger for fear of "rocking the boat" and losing the overvalued partner. Indeed, the patient is often unaware of feeling anger, responding to

---

Table 4–3.   Outline of IPT-D goals and techniques: intermediate
sessions—interpersonal disputes

A. Goals

1. Identify dispute

2. Choose plan of action

3. Modify expectations or faulty communication to bring about a satisfactory resolution

B. Strategies

1. Review depressive symptoms

2. Relate symptom onset to overt or covert dispute with significant other with whom patient is currently involved

a. Search for transgressions in relationship

3. Determine stage of dispute

a. Renegotiation (calm participants)

b. Impasse (increase disharmony to reopen negotiation)

c. Dissolution (assist mourning)

4. Explore how nonreciprocal role expectations contribute to dispute

a. What are the issues in the dispute?

b. What are differences in expectations and values?

c. What are the options?

d. What is the likelihood of finding alternatives?

e. What resources are available to bring about change in the relationship?

5. Are there parallels in other relationships?

a. What is the patient gaining?

b. What unspoken assumptions lie behind the patient's behavior?

6. How is the dispute perpetuated?

a. Inability to express anger, excessive guilt, caretaking role, etc.

7. How does chronic depression affect the patient's behaviors and choices?

---

upsetting situations instead with guilt and self-criticism rather than rage. This "retroflexed rage" often results in a masochistic relationship wherein the patient, unwilling to risk setting limits, silently suffers the partner's hurtful behaviors. Dysthymic patients frequently have histories of childhood and latter day traumata (Akiskal et al. 1981; Kaufman 1991; Klein et al. 1988) to which they respond with guilt rather than anger.

A principle of IPT is that an appropriately outraged, morally justified response to the transgressions of others may be clinically beneficial. The IPT therapist should focus on this disequilibrium, helping the patient to explore his or her needs in sessions and to begin to assert them in the relationship. The goal is not simply abreaction and catharsis, which do not in themselves alter interpersonal functioning, but rather the linking of affect to a specific interpersonal situation.

> What would you have wanted your husband to do? What do you expect from him? How did you feel when he didn't (and let you down)?

Patients are frequently amazed at their newfound power to control the events in their lives and to alter not only their own but their partners' behaviors simply by expressing their feelings. One reported her surprise that it "felt good" when she finally dared "rock the boat" by disagreeing with her boyfriend, who then changed his offensive behavior rather than leaving her as she had anticipated.

> Ms. D, a 32-year-old, single white journalist, reported having felt depressed since early adolescence, even before a teenage trauma after which she felt undeserved guilt for the death of a friend. She had had a series of unsatisfying relationships with men, whom she felt took advantage of her; she "stayed with them too long" lest she feel alone and unmarriageable. When she began dating, shortly after therapy started, she foresaw nothing but disaster in her boyfriend's behavior. She was loath to discuss her feelings and wishes with him for fear of seeming either "too interested" or "too pushy" and losing him. She was subsequently delighted to discover that she could alter the relationship in positive directions simply by expressing her reactions to behaviors she found bothersome—which he then promptly ceased. Even anger, which had previously been taboo, she gradually recognized as a useful and increasingly comfortable emotion. The relationship evolved and her symptoms almost entirely disappeared.

Transgressions of trust.   There are unwritten codes for relationships, reasonable expectations partners have of one another. Because dysthymic individuals are averse to expressing anger, they are at particular risk for being transgressed against. A special type of interpersonal dispute results from transgressions. A transgression occurs when a partner breaks the explicit or implicit rules of a relationship; usually this involves a breach of trust, a sexual or financial indiscretion. Sexual infidelity is probably the most common interpersonal transgression. Sexual abuse of children is another example.

A crucial therapeutic point is that the victim needs to challenge the transgressor and assert his or her moral right to justice. The therapeutic goal with such patients is not simply catharsis but mobilization of anger toward the transgressor who has betrayed their expectations. For dysthymic patients this challenge, fighting back, can be a novel, initially frightening, but ultimately exhilarating experience. The case of Ms. B, cited previously in this chapter, is an example. In short, the recognition of transgressions can be a helpful catalyst for dysthymic patients, galvanizing them through moral right into an active, righteous stance they otherwise might not take. And because dysthymic patients tend to be passive and taken advantage of in relationships, transgressions are often not difficult for the therapist to find.

In subtyping interpersonal disputes, therapists should note whether they concern transgressions, whether they have reached an impasse, and whether they involve 1) sexual issues, 2) financial responsibilities, 3) revelation of a secret, 4) authority/dominance issues, 5) becoming involved or separated in a relationship, 6) child rearing, or 7) other conflicts.

Role Transitions

Role transitions are defined as difficulties in coping with life changes that require a change in one's social or occupational status or self-view. Examples include development of an illness, graduation from school, job change, promotion or demotion, moving to a new city, bachelorhood in the aftermath of divorce, or prolonged alcohol abstinence after years of dependence. Whereas dysthymic patients are likely to emphasize the negative aspects of any change, the therapist can help them recognize actual and potential gains.

> Any transition is a stress, which can have its negative side but almost always has positive aspects as well.

The treatment of this broadly elastic category was reviewed in Chapter 3. Most changes are not absolutely good or bad; to the depressed patient, however, the bad will always appear to outweigh the good. The therapist helps the patient recognize that he or she is undergoing a period of change that can be dealt with, that need not be as chaotic as it feels to the depressed patient (see Table 4–4). Handling the role transition involves recognizing the loss of the old role that existed prior to whatever life event defines the role transition. While mourning that loss, the patient should also come to see the limitations of the old role. At the same time, the therapist can help the patient recognize that the new role may have advantages as well as problems, and that mastery of aspects of the new role may bring those advantages into the patient's actual grasp.

Treatment as transition. A novel strategy, worth pursuing with patients who lack obvious role disputes or complicated bereavements and preferable to focusing on interpersonal deficits alone, is to consider the diagnosis of dysthymic disorder and its treatment (i.e., the assumption of the sick role) as a transition. In most cases the patient, albeit suffering from dysthymic disorder for the remembered decades of his or her life, has not previously received the diagnosis of dysthymic disorder or realized that it is treatable. Previous psychotherapists will frequently have missed the diagnosis, and the patient will tend to view the problem as characterological. This approach charges the IPT treatment with added excitement and may help the patient to feel newly empowered.

> Ms. E, a 43-year-old, married interior decorator, presented with lifelong depression, masochistic and borderline personality traits, and a Ham-D score of 17. She felt especially worthless at times when she was not working, which had become frequent during the economic recession. She and her husband had sexual problems, and she had a difficult relationship with an angry, narcissistic mother. She was skeptical when her therapist diagnosed dysthymic

---

Table 4–4. Outline of IPT-D goals and techniques: intermediate sessions—role transitions

A. Goals

  1. Mourning and acceptance of the loss of the old role

  2. Helping the patient regard the new role as more positive

  3. Building self-esteem by developing a sense of mastery over demands of new roles

B. Strategies

  1. Review depressive symptoms

  2. Relate depressive symptoms to difficulty in coping with recent life change

    a. Diagnosis of dysthymic disorder as a role transition

  3. Review positive and negative aspects of old and new roles

  4. Explore feelings about what is lost

  5. Explore feelings about the change itself

  6. Explore opportunities in the new role

  7. Realistically evaluate what is lost

  8. Encourage appropriate release of affect

  9. Encourage development of social support system and of new skills necessary to the new role

disorder and announced an intratreatment role transition; she tended to see herself as having a melancholic, or even a "borderline" character. She nonetheless tried to "follow the program."

This involved tolerating the anxiety of taking greater interpersonal risks with friends and prospective clients, discussing intimacy with her husband and exploring options in their relationship, making new friends to replace some who had moved away and making attempts to reopen contact with those who had left, and considering buying a dog. Aside from setting limits with her mother, the therapy did not dwell on that relationship or its history. Her Ham-D score dropped to 5. She gradually became convinced of the effect of events on her mood and her ability to exert some control over both ("a blessing"), maintaining her gains in excess of 2½ years in monthly follow-up sessions. It took close to a year before she truly began to believe that she had been suffering from dysthymic disorder rather than character defects.

Interpersonal Deficits

Interpersonal deficits represents the problem area of last resort. Any of the other three problem areas makes a preferable focus; as discussed above, role transition can and should be invoked instead. Yet because most dysthymic patients have such deficits, techniques from this section may be helpful in treating patients whose focus is on other problem areas (see Table 4–5). These deficits may predispose to depression and hinder recovery (Charney et al. 1981; Shea et al. 1990). Patients with interpersonal deficits are the most difficult to treat with IPT, in part because the paucity of relationships limits interpersonal material for therapy. Again, "characterological

---

Table 4–5.   Outline of IPT-D goals and techniques: intermediate
                  sessions—interpersonal deficits

A. Goals

  1. Reduce the patient's social isolation

  2. Encourage formation of new relationships

B. Strategies

  1. Review depressive symptoms

  2. Relate depressive symptoms to problems of social isolation or unfulfillment

  3. Review past significant relationships including their negative and positive aspects

  4. Explore repetitive patterns in relationships

  5. Discuss patient's positive and negative feelings about therapist and seek parallels in other relationships

---

deficits" are difficult to gauge in the presence of a mood disorder. Particularly depressively tinged avoidant, dependent, or self-defeating traits may represent facets of chronic depression rather than comorbid personality disorders.

Because interpersonal difficulties associated with dysthymic disorder may be mood-related, vigorous treatment with IPT may both alleviate depressive symptoms and simultaneously challenge affectively tinged beliefs and behaviors. For dysthymic patients, the difficulties typically involve 1) social isolation, 2) anxious inhibition, 3) sense of inadequacy, 4) lack of self-assertion, 5) guilty inability to express anger, and 6) inhibited social risk taking. Each of these is discussed in the following section.

Issues of "Character"

As noted, many dysthymic patients meet criteria for axis II personality disorders, particularly masochistic (self-defeating), avoidant, and dependent types. It is unclear how much of this is trait and how much the "chronic state" of persistent mood disorder, particularly because all the above character types have traits that are affectively laden. The axis II disorder may disappear as dysthymic disorder lifts.

For the purposes of treatment it is useful to discuss with patients that what they think of as their "personality" may not be that at all; an explicit aim of IPT-D, particularly when the focus is the iatrogenic role transition of the dysthymic diagnosis, is to lift the mood and find out what the patient is "really" like when not depressed. It is a great and exciting boon for patients to discover not only that their depression is treatable but that they have a new lease on character as well. (The goal of IPT-D is not to change character but often to uncover latent character beneath chronic depression.) Usually an important aspect of treatment is the *"normalizing" of emotional reactions that dysthymic patients tend to see as "bad," especially anxiety and anger.* Here follow some common quasicharacterologic issues.

Social isolation.   The therapist addresses social isolation by encouraging occupational and extraoccupational activities. "What did you do over the weekend?" often yields revealing answers. Social activities allow testing and reworking of interpersonal patterns. Dysthymic patients are often slow to recognize or to report pleasurable activities, some of which they may have abandoned years before and forgotten. Hobbies, particularly social activities that bring the patient into contact with others, should be encouraged. Whatever the outcome of such activities, they provide opportunities to examine social behaviors, expectations, and desires. Patients are often surprised to find things have gone better than expected. One patient reclaimed her youthful interest in pottery, which led to her making friends with people who had similar interests. Encouraging the same patient to go out with office colleagues also resulted in unexpected pleasure.

Treatment strategy: The therapist should note the explicit antidepressant benefits of activity which, as noted above, counter the feeling that the patient is worthless and "not doing anything." On the other hand, the therapist must help assess whether the patient is setting realistic goals. In the context of the sick role, the therapist can also reassure the patient that he or she is "fighting with one hand tied behind your back" and need not set perfectionistic standards for his or her performance. The effort to explore one's options is always worth making, even if a particular attempt turns out to be not entirely successful, because successes and failures can help the patient discover a richer, happier, euthymic adjustment.

Anxious inhibition.   Avoidant and dependent dysthymic patients tend to have fragile and timorous self-images. In working with these patients, the therapist frequently takes a "carrot-and-stick" approach, both supporting and gently spurring the patient forward into anxiety-provoking new interpersonal terrain. These patients may have difficulty even considering self-assertive options or may comfort themselves with the sense that their timid behaviors are in fact aggressive.

> Ms. F felt that she was assertive and noted that others in her family described her as "the outspoken one." Yet this patient was chronically unable to prevent her extended family from making lengthy stays (of several years) in her apartment. Her example of her assertiveness was an occasion when a visiting sister overheard the patient bemoaning her fate during a telephone call and asked whether the patient wanted her to end her visit. The patient then gave an equivocal reply, in effect diminishing a golden opportunity.
>
> In this instance, formulated as a role dispute between the patient and her live-in relatives, the therapist both congratulated the patient for being "the outspoken one" and analyzed her communication patterns, exploring alternative options to help the patient develop (still) more effective ways of confronting and setting limits with her family.

Role playing with the therapist at this juncture might have helped Ms. F prepare for more effective self-assertion outside the office.

Similarly, a dependent patient who was unable to conceive of leaving a depressingly unequal relationship was encouraged to think through the consequences of a "trial separation" analogous to a work leave she was taking because of her depression. Just considering the option of leaving, supported and elaborated by role play during sessions, was sufficient to change her way of relating to her partner, leading to improvement in mood and relationship.

The limiting factor for self-assertion for an avoidance patient is typically the anxiety of humiliation and for the dependent patient the anxiety of desertion and aloneness. Guilty anxiety hounds these "masochistic" patients and what might be called pseudoaltruism—the rationalization of putting other people's needs first, used by the avoidant Ms. F above. Pseudoaltruism should be contrasted with healthy self-ishness (see Self-assertion, pp. 109–110). The therapist needs to explore not only what the patient wants but why. Does a patient maintain a relationship or change residences because it is in his or her own best interest to do so, or because it avoids unpleasant confrontation and is in fact to someone else's advantage?

Treatment strategy: Whichever the apparent personality traits—and they often overlap—the therapist's goals are to

1. Point out the maladaptive behavior to the patient
2. Define the behavior as a chronic symptom resulting from and maintained by dysthymic disorder
3. Help the patient consider alternative behaviors (i.e., explore options) based on what the patient wants in life
4. Encourage the patient to test these behaviors in life outside the session

Dysthymic patients frequently describe "personality-disordered" avoidant, dependent, or masochistic interactions with the resigned explanation, "That's the way I am." To which the response is

> That's the way you've *been*. When you've been depressed long enough, it's hard to tell what's you—your personality—and how much is depression influencing your character. You have dysthymic disorder, which interferes with your interactions with people. But now that you're becoming aware of it, it doesn't have to interfere. The more you act with others in ways that aren't depressed, the better you're going to feel.

It is useful to explore this in minor interpersonal situations (confronting a rude stranger in a bank line), explicitly building up to the more overwhelming ones (e.g., leaving a bad marriage).

Sense of inadequacy and lack of self-worth (if not worthlessness). Too often the patients' efforts have been expended in the pursuit of conformity, to blend in and not be noticed lest they be recognized as inadequate, unlovable, or strange.

They feel bad about themselves if they avoid interaction, yet like "frauds" even when they interact successfully because this means hiding their inner sense of worthlessness. It is a no-win situation. The sense of inadequacy emerges particularly when the patient approaches a relationship that could involve intimacy. Self-image in these social situations is invariably distorted, with the patient's perception far worse than warranted. IPT can help patients examine their reactions in interpersonal contexts.

Patients fear dating lest they be rejected, as they feel they are boring, uninteresting, and defective. Avoidant, seeking conformity, many are "wallflowers" who dress conservatively and feel inexperienced in social and sexual intercourse. Many lack knowledge of how to demonstrate their interest in or affection to others.

> Ms. G, a 29-year-old woman, reported lifelong dysthymic disorder and the sense she was unlovable and defective. She had dared hope only for (masochistic) sexual encounters, not relationships. In IPT-D she was encouraged to become involved with an office co-worker whom she found attractive and with whom she had long been friendly. She found this relationship sexually and emotionally more satisfying than any previous one. She was surprised to learn from her new lover that until her behavior changed he had never recognized the intent of the previously limited expressions of interest she had been able to muster and had always regarded her as simply friendly, "one of the boys" at the office.

Treatment strategy: The therapist needs to convince the patient that the illness of dysthymic disorder, not some inherent lack of self-worth or shyness, is the source of the patient's discomfort. DSM-IV (American Psychiatric Association 1994), which lists low self-esteem as a dysthymic symptom, may be helpful (see Table 1–1).

> Dysthymic disorder makes you think you can't handle your social role in these situations, but let's prepare ahead of time and then see how you really can do. You just need to build up your confidence that you can handle these social situations, get some practice in them, and then they'll seem a lot less scary.

This simply restates the basic premise of IPT.

In accord with the IPT-D approach of challenging patients to reconceptualize their self-view, the question of "fraudulence" deserves scrutiny. If a dysthymic patient succeeds in a social or occupational situation but then dismisses this as "fraud," the dysthymic disorder is doing that patient a disservice, discounting any credit for the achievement. The therapist might comment,

> I understand you *feel* like a fraud—it's one of the most common things I hear from dysthymic patients, almost a proof of the diagnosis! But this is the dysthymic disorder cheating you of an accomplishment. It seems to me that what this shows is that *you have the capacity to succeed* [to talk to people, finish an assignment well, etc.] *despite* the depression that's holding you back. You're not a fraud; dysthymic disorder just makes you feel that way. This makes me wonder how much still better you'll be able to function as the depressive symptoms fade.

Patients frequently are pleased to find that asking and knowing are better than withdrawing and guessing at others' motives. Taking the risk of being rejected can lead to their being accepted; with acceptance may come erosion of the inner sense of defectiveness, the ineffable depressive "fatal flaw." In contrast, nothing can be won if risks are not taken. One patient's comment paraphrases the feelings of many: "I'm learning that if I try, it's scary, but things may turn out okay."

Self-assertion.   Dysthymic disorder makes martyrs. I do not mean this cavalierly. Years of chronic depression eroding self-assertion can make it appear selfish to want anything for oneself. Many patients feel almost constitutionally unable to get angry. To object to the wishes of others seems "petty" when they can guiltily accede; but they feel far too guilty to act on their own wishes, particularly if these conflict with anyone else's.

Almost to a one, then, dysthymic individuals suffer from passivity, lack of self-assertion, fear of risk-taking, and social embarrassment. There is a chronic sense of living at the mercy of one's mood and a self-sacrificing tendency to devote oneself to the needs of others. By expressing needs to others, dysthymic patients may learn that they can indeed control their internal and external environments, affecting both the feelings within and the behavior of those around them.

Dysthymic individuals may shun promotions and avoid work that entails social confidence lest they prove inadequate to the stress and attention. They often have difficulties with the social culture of the job milieu, as opposed to paperwork and other asocial aspects of work. Yet by and large they are excellent, if overly self-critical, workers. The therapist should help the patient explore successes at work, how supervisors and others perceive them, and encourage reevaluation of their self-esteem and goals in light of this.

Treatment strategy: A careful discussion of the patient's interpersonal environment often makes plain that, for example, they may deserve a raise. The therapist may need to explain to the patient, in a simple, straightforward way, that a certain amount of selfishness is healthy.

> Doesn't it seem that you're entitled to a raise? Is it really unhealthily "selfish" to want what you deserve? When you're depressed it can be hard to feel that you deserve much of anything.

The next step is to suggest that dysthymic disorder has eroded or inhibited the development of self-assertion.

> It's not good to do anything to an extreme; you don't want to be selfish all the time, but you don't want to be completely self*less*, either—then you never get what you want. Let's see if we can help you strike a healthy balance. Because of your dysthymic disorder, you're at great risk for being too selfless and for not expressing a healthy degree of self-interest.

Some dysthymic patients may fear that if they gratify one "selfish" wish, they will act selfishly all the time. Therapists can provide reassurance that their danger lies at the other end of the spectrum, in not being selfish enough.

If the patient agrees on the goal of asking for a raise (or a date, or whatever), the next step is to help the patient explore the options for getting it. Role playing often helps the patient to develop the phrasing, the tone of voice, and to plan the setting and contingencies surrounding the attempt at self-assertion. It is frequently wise to plan a test run in a less charged area (i.e., a hierarchy of tasks) so that the patient can bring some success experience to the more important and seemingly dangerous area.

Guilty inability to express anger.   Dysthymic people find it much easier to get guilty than angry—retroflexed rage, perhaps (see also Interpersonal Role Dispute, pp. 99–102). Anger is frequently viewed as a "bad," unworthy emotion. Inability to express anger appropriately puts dysthymic patients at the mercy of their environment, at risk for abuse that they then compound with guilty self-blame. This is most obvious in evidently self-defeating dysthymic patients but can be seen in most who have dysthymic disorder—even in those (relatively rare) patients who can mount some kind of angry retort. Inability to express anger appropriately is a crucial interpersonal impairment for dysthymic patients.

Treatment strategy:

1. Borrowing a page from cognitive-behavior therapy, which educates anxious patients about anxiety as a biological response, the IPT-D therapist provides

psychoeducation by describing anger as a *normal*, inborn response to noxious events in the environment (i.e., anger can be helpful and useful in alerting the patient to things going wrong and mistreatment by others).

2. A corollary: although the dysthymic patient feels "bad," identifies anger as a "bad" feeling, and senses that this "badness" comes from within, sometimes the problem is external, in the environment, interpersonal. No matter how great the justification for anger, many dysthymic patients tend to feel that expressing anger is "being a bitch." It's important to help the patient distinguish between depression and oppression.

> Sometimes you feel angry because someone's hurt you. Anger isn't a bad feeling that comes from within; it tells you when someone's bothering you. It's normal and useful to be angry in this situation. It's not a comfortable feeling, but it's a useful one. It's good to know when someone is stepping on your toe—and [your friend] is.

This clarification, helping the patient to distinguish him- or herself from the offending other in an emotionally murky situation, often requires repetition to convince.

3. In addition to detoxifying anger as a "bad" emotion, the therapist often has to address the patient's overvaluation of the danger of anger: the fear of losing control, embarrassing oneself, or of killing others.
4. With practice, patients often find the expression of anger a liberating experience and a key definition of self against the environment—particularly if this is catalyzed in the context of redressing a transgression (q.v.), resolving a role dispute, etc. Because of the chronicity of dysthymia, a novel behavior such as standing up to a longtime bully, boss, or spouse provides dramatic proof of improvement to both the patient and those around him or her. Bullies often back off; disputes are resolved.
5. Keys to expressing anger appropriately include the following:
   a. *Addressing a specific focus.* Global anger is disorganizing and frightening for patients. Dredging up other issues may lead a patient past the current situation that he or she most needs to address.
   b. *Addressing a problem in the here and now.* That is, the anger should address an issue with current emotional valence. Because the patient may have avoided anger in important relationships for years, anger will frequently have something to do with past events, especially when dealing with grief.
   c. *A clear outcome in the patient's mind.* What are the patient's expectations about expressing anger and its consequences? What are the consequences of not getting angry?

d. *Role playing.* Role playing with the therapist often helps the patient practice what he or she wants to say, an appropriate tone of voice, etc.

Occasionally dysthymic patients have the opposite problem; they do register anger but are so afraid of exploding that they go to the opposite extreme and are fearful of expressing any objection. Mr. H, a dysthymic patient who had a history of fighting and abusive behavior on rare occasions when he allowed himself to drink, became abstinent from alcohol. He was subsequently afraid to approach any situation that evoked anger lest he again "explode," although there was nothing to suggest he would do this when sober:

> *Therapist:* Feelings that feel painful when you are depressed can be normal and useful emotions that tell you about your environment and how to react to it. Like sadness and anger.
>
> *H:* I'm afraid of going to see my family because I'll get too upset if I see them.
>
> *T:* We've talked about this before; you mean you're afraid you'll get angry, and you don't want to explode. You would rather go through life not getting angry, but that's impossible. Rather, it's important to get comfortable with anger, handle it appropriately. Have you discussed your feelings with your wife?
>
> *H:* Yes, I was surprised at her sympathy.
>
> *T:* So tell me how you feel about your family and what you'd like to say to them. Maybe we can find a "safe" way for you to get these feelings off your chest and yet have everyone survive.

Role playing with the therapist subsequently prepared Mr. H to meet his family and to verbalize his anger in a controlled, effective manner.

Social risk taking. The social discomforts we all feel are compounded by dysthymic disorder. Dysthymic individuals accordingly tend to avoid such seemingly dangerous situations. Yet risk taking often leads to what George Brown has called "fresh new starts": positive life events that empower and remoralize depressed patients (Brown and Harris 1978). Unless and until patients are willing to take such risks, they cannot know their true, euthymic capacities. Taking social risks, and succeeding in them, may play an important role in how IPT helps patients to recover from their depressive illness.

Expressing anger and asserting oneself are particular examples of a range of social risk taking. An important agenda for dysthymic patients is to learn to welcome rather than to fear such social risks. An example of risk taking might be taking a vacation; many dysthymic individuals are desperately hard workers who do not dare use their vacation days, do not feel they deserve a vacation, and fear going somewhere new. Taking such a break may help to challenge these depressive assumptions while allowing the patient to have a good time.

Risk taking can also involve choosing a new relationship or career trajectory. Whether patients appear avoidant, dependent, or masochistic, risk taking is frequently a difficulty.

Treatment strategy: The approach to this issue is to point out that risk taking is anxiety provoking for everyone (no one likes to be turned down for a date) but that when you are chronically depressed it gets that much harder. Nonetheless, not taking chances means missing opportunities, being cut off from others. It thus compounds the isolation and fatalism of dysthymic disorder.

> Dysthymic disorder makes taking chances seem riskier than it is. Anxiety and indecisiveness are symptoms of your depression; dysthymic disorder saps your energy and confidence, discourages you. As we've been talking I've gotten the impression that you are more frightened than you need be and that it holds you back. Let's look at your expectations about how others will react if you should take such risks.

Taking risks—reasonable risks, not truly dangerous ones—is one way to gain control of situations and to help oneself feel better.

> Everyone has blind spots; you may err on the side of caution. Some risks are dangerous and not worth taking, others a bit dangerous but worth taking.

This has particular utility for role transitions, when patients are invariably confronting the "risks" of new situations.

Confrontations of any kind are uncomfortable for dysthymic patients. Yet if we define confrontations as interpersonal situations where one expresses one's feelings, they are a necessary part of daily life. In IPT-D, dysthymic patients learn to see confrontations not as horrible situations to be avoided at all costs but rather as useful opportunities to let other people know what they want (and do not want) and how they feel.

Overall, it takes time to "build a new track record" after years of dysthymic disorder. The therapist can provide reassurance, based on clinical experience, that it takes time for a new vision to sink in.

Keeping a Therapeutic Equilibrium

It is not always easy for the IPT-D therapist to maintain the positive, optimistic stance I suggest. Dysthymic patients can be draining and exhausting; the therapists in our study agree that they are harder to work with than acutely depressed patients but not impossible. It is important to keep countertransference in check, not to blame the patient for the illness, and to remind oneself that the goal of euthymia is achievable. The pessimism the therapist may feel at times largely reflects the patient's own despair rather than a realistic appraisal of the patient's prognosis. There is hope!

The therapists in our dysthymia study felt overwhelmed when they met their first patients. In supervision they questioned whether IPT-D would work with the efficacy IPT has shown for major depression. By the end of their 16-week treatments, however, they were pleasantly surprised, convinced by the results they saw. If you as a therapist maintain your hope and pursue your therapeutic options, the patient has hope and options too. IPT helps therapists to maintain hope by providing a structure for treatment and therapeutic options to fall back on. You and the patient (the potentially healthy patient, as opposed to his or her dysthymia) can supply the rest. If you can help the patient gain skills and change difficult life situations, he or she is very likely to feel better.

Final Sessions (Sessions 13 to 16–18)

Termination

In terminating acute treatment, the patient is asked to give up the relationship with the therapist as the patient moves toward recognition of his or her independent competence to deal with problem areas. The IPT therapist announces termination at least three or four sessions before the end and subsequently elicits patient responses to it. Termination should be recognized as a time of potential sadness but also a graduation from the sick role (back) to social competence. In these last sessions the therapist and patient should review key interpersonal issues, consolidate gains made, and appreciate the success of their alliance while lamenting its ending.

Although patients who respond to IPT-D should continue to receive a continuation or maintenance form of the treatment, it is important that the therapist demarcate the end of acute treatment as a time to consolidate gains. The monthly booster sessions represent a significant dilution of therapist contact. Termination should not be minimized by the presence of these continuation sessions on the horizon.

Dysthymic patients, tending to overvalue the importance of others in relationships and to underrate themselves, are often reluctant to end therapy after 4 months. The therapist must help the patient to appreciate both the degree to which they have improved and the patient's own responsibility and credit for that improvement.

> We've accomplished a lot in a brief time. I want to point out that this wasn't magic; you've gotten out of depression and dramatically changed your relationships and outlook because of the things you did, the risks you took.

Given the chronicity of their illness, patients should be encouraged to keep working on these same issues after therapy ends.

> Now that you recognize what you've been dealing with all your life, you know what to do. Continuing to address these issues—expressing your wishes and your anger to your boyfriend where appropriate, risking asking for the raise you deserve—is likely both to keep you from being depressed and make you ever more comfortable in those interpersonal situations.

> It takes time to build a new track record in your new, nondepressed state, to really build confidence in yourself.

The termination phase of IPT should counter fears of relapse by reviewing the symptoms of depression, summarizing the problem area and how the patient has addressed it, and suggesting that he or she may be able to do the same with his or her newly acquired skills should new problems arise in the future. Patients should leave with the knowledge that they always do have options, even if depression seems to mask them, and that by dealing with the interpersonal issues that have given them difficulty in the past, they may avert depression in the future.

Continuation and Maintenance Sessions

See Chapter 8.

IPT-D Techniques

These techniques are identical to those described in the previous chapter.

Facilitation of Affect

Successful therapy involves acknowledgment of painful affects surrounding interpersonal issues as well as encouragement of new emotional experiences to facilitate growth and change. Mobilization of affect and catharsis are insufficient per se in treating depression. So is an affectively detached, intellectualized discussion of an interpersonal problem area. Therapists should look and pull for affect as a determining focus of sessions, leading therapist and patient to the interpersonal issues worth exploring.

As the patient's depressive affect gradually gives way to euthymia in the course of effective therapy, anger and self-criticism ("retroflexed rage") that the patient had previously focused on him- or herself may belatedly be turned toward others who took advantage of their depression, avenging transgressions, etc. Several patients were initially embarrassed at what they felt was "childish" anger but with support found it a useful impetus to mobilize changes in their relationships with lovers, business clientele, etc. "Better angry than depressed," remarked one. In addition to anger, a genuine sadness emerges as depression clears. As discussed above, the expression of anger toward others is of particular importance for dysthymic patients.

Encouraging Activity and Socialization

As Robert Burton wrote in *The Anatomy of Melancholy* (1621/1948), "Be not solitary, be not idle" (p. 970). The goal is not just "keeping busy"; getting the patient out of bed and out of the house achieves several functions. Activity demonstrates to patients that they are more capable than their depression leads them to believe, providing a sense of accomplishment and overcoming depressive premonitions of failure. So long as plans are not so ambitious as to invite failure and self-recrimination, activity is antidepressant relative to isolation and rumination. Moreover, activity increases the opportunity for interpersonal interactions, creating more material for therapy.

Explore Options

Hopelessness, a characteristic feature of depression, leads to underestimation of one's capabilities and options in life. This is particularly so for dysthymic patients, who may have always felt their future foreclosed. An important aspect of IPT is the examination of realistic life goals for patients, clarifying in the process how depression has temporarily blinded them from seeing genuine opportunities. "What do you want?" is a key question, one that many dysthymic patients may have long before stopped considering. Part of the recovery process is indeed helping dysthymic patients to consider what they might want and how to pursue it.

Clarification

Also important is clarification of the therapist's simple delineation of the patient's interpersonal relationship or pattern of relationships. This should generally be linked to depressive affect (see Klerman et al. 1984).

Communication Analysis

Many dysthymic patients misinterpret interpersonal encounters based on their social hypersensitivity. Benign remarks may be interpreted as rejections. Therapists should endeavor to learn the details of conversations the patient has had with others and to review both what has transpired and what options the patient might have had, or might still have, to ameliorate such encounters (see Klerman et al. 1984).

Use of Therapeutic Relationship

This is generally restricted to patients whose problem area is interpersonal deficits. Although the focus of IPT is on relationships outside the office, for isolated patients who lack such relationships the therapeutic relationship becomes a focus by default. The therapist's goal is to emphasize the benign aspects of this interaction with an eye to encouraging the patient to risk interpersonal contacts with others.

Summary at End of Session

It is important to consolidate and underscore gains at the end of each session and periodically to restate the interpersonal focus of the therapy.

Special Situations

Often treatment is sought for an acute precipitant. Some dysthymic patients may seek treatment because depressive symptoms have been inflamed by an acute stressor. The patient seeks relief from this immediate distress but may be less willing to address changing overall functioning and self-view, having so insidious and chronic an affective disorder that he or she is inured to it. Defensiveness, protests of helplessness, hopelessness, and vulnerability may arise when the therapist proposes changes in chronic maladaptive interpersonal behaviors and relationships. Social withdrawal and isolation may contribute to dysthymic disorder, but the patient may also perceive them as protection against rejection, external criticism, and abandonment that are viewed as worse than the dysthymic status quo.

Motivation for change may be enhanced by successful application of IPT-D to dispel distress associated with an acute problem area, such as grief or a role dispute. Yet some dysthymic patients may be inclined to terminate treatment once the acute distress improves. Hence psychoeducation about dysthymic disorder and its treatment is important during initial sessions, with reinforcement throughout the course of IPT-D as needed, to ensure treatment of the chronic affective disorder.

CHAPTER 5
CASE EXAMPLES

Past cure I am, now Reason is past care,
And frantic-mad with evermore unrest.

—William Shakespeare,
Sonnet 147

Past hope, past cure, past help!

—William Shakespeare,
Romeo and Juliet

S hakespeare's words capture the desperation many dysthymic patients experience, but happily we now have effective treatments for dysthymic disorder. The cases that follow describe the
psychopathology of typical dysthymic patients, some of the issues that arise in the
course of treatment, and specific interpersonal psychotherapy (IPT) interventions,
and their outcome. Sometimes the cases that look the hardest are not. Cases mentioned in IPT training workshops are frequently dysthymic patients; when reconsidered from the IPT perspective, the cases often look more approachable to the
therapists who have cited them.

Role Playing Self-Assertion and
the Expression of Anger

Ms. J, a 53-year-old, married saleswoman in an art gallery, reported lifelong dysthymic disorder. "I'm useless," she said, "Just waiting to die." Raised in an emotionally frigid family, she had married unhappily in her late teens in an attempt to escape her family of origin. Her relationship with her husband was distant, asexual, and angry, but she felt too incapable and incompetent to even consider leaving him. She also felt incompetent socially and at work. She could not recall ever feeling happy or capable. Ms. J had had lengthy treatment with psychodynamic psychotherapy, which had provided some fleeting insights but no relief, and with antidepressant medication, which had produced little response even at high doses. She was dubious about the IPT for dysthymic disorder (IPT-D) definition of her problem as a medical mood disorder but conceded that this was at least a fresh view of things. Her initial Hamilton Depression Rating Scale (Ham-D) (Hamilton 1960) score was 24 on the 24-item version of the scale (significantly depressed). She was passively suicidal but had made no plans or attempts ("I'd only mess it up").

The therapist gave a version of the usual IPT-D formulation:

> I don't think you're useless, you just have a medical illness, dysthymic disorder, that makes you feel that way. You've had it for so long that of course it feels like part of you, but it doesn't have to be that way. I would like to spend the next 16 weeks with you working on a *role transition* in which you move from accepting the depression as part of yourself to distinguishing between depression and your healthy self. If you can do that, you're pretty much bound to feel better and more capable.

Therapy thus focused on the role transition of recognizing her "real" personality in contrast to dysthymic symptoms and on expanding her interpersonal repertoire in her relationships with others. She acknowledged her anger at her husband (a role dispute), felt there was no resolving the chronic role dispute between them, and looked into the possibility of moving out but without much conviction. At the same time, she and the therapist worked on her interactions with co-workers. She had been particularly upset by her interactions with a rude, competitive colleague who interrupted her when she was helping customers.

> *Ms. J:* Rose is rude, interrupts me when I'm dealing with patrons. I don't like her at all.

Therapist: That sounds understandable. What can you do?

J: I'm not good at doing anything . . . . I don't feel very effective . . . . Is there a book I can read on how to be effective?

T: We'll write it right now. Do you feel that it's appropriate for you to be annoyed? I mean, do you feel Rose is genuinely annoying?

J: I never know if it's me or the other person, but I think some other people have been bothered by her too, even though she often comes across as sweet.

T: So if it's reasonable to feel angry, what can you say to Rose?

J: "Excuse me, I'll talk to you later?"

T: Does that get across what you want to say? How do you feel? What do you feel like saying?

J: I feel like telling her to learn some manners!

T: Okay, fine! That sounds right, that makes sense to me; but it's a little blunt. Is there another way to put that? Is there a more direct way to tell her *why* you want her to learn some manners?

J: I'd like to tell her that it's rude to interrupt, that if she waits I'll get back to her, but that she shouldn't break in.

T: Fine! Now pretend I'm Rose and say it to me . . . .

Note that this interchange tended to normalize anger as an appropriate response for the patient in noxious interpersonal situations.

With role playing, Ms. J was able to express her resentment. This led her to raise the problem of Frank, a man whose time was supposed to be split between working for Ms. J and for Rose.

J: But after I told him to do some things, Rose told him to do hers first.

T: [Astounded] What was your response to that?

J: I didn't say anything, wasn't sure if it was true or just what Frank was telling me.

T: You're right, it's good to figure that out. But if Rose really said that, how would you feel?

J: Annoyed . . .

T: Yes, I quite understand! And what could you do, if you felt annoyed?

J: I guess talk to her about it.

T: And what would you want to say? [After some role playing] . . . The more you can draw the line with people who bother you, the better you're likely to feel: both because you get the anger off your chest and because you put the person who's bothering you on warning. If you don't say anything, it's possible that Rose doesn't know she's being rude or competitive; if you say something, she has no excuse to keep doing it.

Ms. J returned the following week and reported that she had confronted Rose when Rose interrupted a conversation with their common boss: "I'm busy with Ellen right now. I'll talk to you later." Although Rose didn't exactly stop talking, Ellen then supported Ms. J by telling Rose to wait in the next room.

T: So how did you feel?

J: Okay; maybe I shouldn't have raised my voice?

T: Tell me how your voice sounded. [She mimicked herself] . . . That doesn't sound like you raised your voice too much. It's sometimes more effective to show a little feeling in your voice if you want to communicate how you feel.

If Ms. J's voice *had* sounded appropriate, I would have congratulated her and encouraged her. Because it wasn't, we eventually did more role playing to refine her technique.

Ms. J conceded feeling some vindication from this encounter. She felt a little guilty, however, and so invited Rose to have some tea. Rose announced: "I didn't bring any money, you'll have to pay for me." As they discussed their relationship, Rose abruptly asked whether Ms. J meant "my manners could stand improvement?" Ms. J said yes, and Rose stormed out.

Ms. J and her therapist agreed that this proved the point about Rose's manners. Ms. J also felt cheered by the encounter, although it was hard for her to pinpoint why.

T: This shows you can have some control over your interactions with other people. And the more you do, the better you're likely to feel.

This discussion with the therapist eventually led to Ms. J raising the difficulties of her marriage, where "I haven't had the courage to leave."

T: If you don't want to leave, then at least you can apply the lesson you've just completed; you can set limits with your husband, too. . . . If I were you I'd feel good about what you've done in talking to Rose!

J: It's hard for me to feel good about anything. But you're right, I'd probably feel less good if I hadn't said something.

T: Your anger would still be on your chest. And now Rose has no excuse for interrupting in future. . . . So you see, you can affect your mood by affecting the interpersonal situations you find yourself in.

Although Ms. J insisted that she was "a slow learner" and unlikely to do anything with her life, in the remaining sessions of the 16-week course of IPT she solidified a shaky sense of social competence at work and began to renegotiate matters with her husband. At the same time, she began looking around for an apartment of her own, with the idea of trying to spend a few months on her own to see whether she could function without her husband. Although she felt "too old to be just starting life at 53," she was taking steps to do so, and her Ham-D score fell to 7, essentially euthymic. In monthly continuation and maintenance sessions she reported that she had neither left her husband nor greatly improved her marriage, but she had a clearer perspective on her role in it, a new appreciation of her husband's failings, and less blame for herself. She put together a resume for new jobs but in the meantime felt new respect from her co-workers and a greater sense of competence in her work.

This case demonstrates how the optimistic, "can-do" approach of IPT can mobilize a doubting patient to action. The therapist supported the patient's feeling of anger, which she had regarded as impotent, and helped her to express it more effectively. For patients whose social skills are shaky, role playing is an important rehearsal of interpersonal skills that can then be used in the world outside the office.

Formulation: Dealing With Dating Situations

Ms. K, a 28-year-old, single bulimic patient with lifelong dysthymic disorder, felt better on fluoxetine 20 mg qd but still somewhat depressed. She felt inadequate in social situations. Her mood varied with her eating and vice versa. She had been in various forms of psychotherapy over the years and tended to intellectualize her situation. Although she was bright, personable, and attractive, she felt fat—an idea reinforced by some chic friends and by her family. She reported that she had just visited her family out of town and that they told her she was fat, as usual.

Therapist: They always do that?

Ms. K: Yes.

T: And how do you respond?

K: I don't say anything. I've never been good at defending myself.

T: Well, it's hard if you've been depressed for a long time. But it's not that hard to learn, with practice, and you feel better, and safer, if you can defend yourself.

K: I feel uncomfortable, then having this feeling of leaden depression, then I pull back . . . in social situations. If I don't like a guy, I go away. If I do like him, I get shy, uncomfortable, and go away. Or I provoke a fight and tell him to fuck off.

T: I see. That's a no-win situation!

K: That's my masochism.

T: You talk about it as if that's a fixed pattern you can't do anything about! But as we've discussed, I think you have dysthymic disorder, not a masochistic character. Maybe there are other things you can do in that situation that would lead you to feel better? . . . When you first came here you just wanted medication. Since you're not having side effects, let's increase it, and more may provide more help. But there are also tricks to solving interpersonal situations so that you feel better in them, can actually control your moods rather than feeling controlled by them. As we've discussed, you have dysthymic disorder, or chronic depression. Your moods and your eating seem to have a lot to do with your relationships with other people and what's happening in your life. I suggest that we use the next 16 weeks to help you distinguish the lifelong depression you've had from *who you are when you're not depressed.*

Ms. K agreed to a combined treatment with pharmacotherapy plus IPT, in which she did quite well. The IPT-D focus was on the role transition out of bulimia and dysthymic disorder and into health. Both her bingeing and purging and her mood improved as she came to understand their determinants in her social life and how she could better handle these. By the third week of treatment she was taking far more "risks" in attending social events, and by midtreatment she was risking dates with men. Although one bad date led to a binge of chocolate, this only helped convince her of the connection between her life events, mood, and food. She was increasingly able to voice what she wanted in social situations and to explore the options to achieve it.

By the end of the 16 weeks of acute treatment she was euthymic and not bingeing or purging. She has maintained her gains in maintenance treatment, which consists of ongoing medication with a serotonin reuptake inhibitor and monthly IPT.

Late-Onset Dysthymic Disorder

Ms. L, a 48-year-old divorced mother of two, denied having been depressed prior to age 40, when she gradually slid into a dysthymic disorder of late onset. Her mood symptoms seemed related to increasing difficulties in her marriage of 15 years. Her husband, a successful businessman, was rarely around and may have been having an affair. When, after more than 3 years, Ms. L developed symptoms of major depression, her husband pushed for her psychiatric hospitalization. While she was in the hospital, he sued for divorce and custody of both children.

Ms. L was eventually discharged from her first psychiatric hospitalization to find herself divorced, stripped of her role as a mother, and branded a sick psychiatric patient; she was given the diagnosis of borderline personality disorder and referred to a long-term treatment unit where she spent almost a year. She signed a paltry divorce settlement. Three years later, she presented for IPT at her long-term psychiatrist's suggestion. In that interval her life seemed to have been on hold; indeed, she felt that it was over and that she had nothing to live for. On presentation, she met criteria for dysthymic disorder but not for borderline personality disorder. There was no history of cutting or self-mutilation, substance abuse, nor a pattern of unstable interpersonal relationships. Her Ham-D score was 28. Ms. L announced at the start her suspicion of psychiatrists, whom she felt had given her little support. (This, surely, is a dispiriting history. Would not many therapists panic or capitulate or settle for very gradual progress?)

Her IPT therapist gave her the diagnosis of dysthymic disorder *as opposed to borderline personality disorder;* as treatment unfolded, the latter seemed more and more clearly a misdiagnosis. The goal of the 16-week IPT treatment was to focus on an iatrogenic role transition; her life had taken a severe turn for the worse several years before, and now in therapy she would learn to regain euthymia to separate herself from the chronic depression that had enveloped her life. A secondary focus was role disputes with her children and with her previous therapists and hospital.

Ms. L spent hours each day ruminating and blaming herself; she seemed to have accepted her husband's divorce charges that she had abandoned her children, who now wanted little to do with her. She had been a failure as a wife and a mother. Her therapist reviewed what had happened in her recent life and helped her consider alternatives: should she be blaming herself, or did her husband deserve some of the blame? And should she perhaps feel some anger toward the doctors and hospital that had given her little support and a punitive diagnosis? As time went on, she came to acknowledge that she had good reason to be angry at others for what had happened to her. This was in no way a disavowal of her own role, and she continued, if anything, to blame herself unduly.

At the same time, Ms. L and her therapist explored what she would like to do with her current life to make it better and happier. Much of this involved reestablishing a maternal role with her children, now teenagers, who followed their father's line in blaming her for having abandoned them. The therapy focused on her growing awareness of her anger at how she had been treated: her husband's manipulation of her worsening depression and her doctor's misdiagnosis of her condition. She began to express her anger and to defend herself: first, role playing, in sessions with the therapist, then in conversations with her children.

Although she had long questioned the diagnosis of borderline personality disorder, she had previously done so in a petulant, ineffective way. Now, backed by her IPT therapist, she confronted her long-term psychiatrist and the hospital about the diagnosis. She sought to have the diagnosis changed in her records. Ms. L reported deriving some satisfaction from addressing and putting to rest a diagnosis she felt had been punitive and stigmatizing.

The 16-week treatment did not eliminate Ms. L's dysthymic symptoms, but it did lower them considerably to a score in the low teens—the best she had been in years. She felt more comfortable in her social roles and seemed to be developing new directions in her life. She also had demonstrated a new, if still shaky, ability to express anger. And she felt a new trust in relationships; her interaction with the IPT therapist was a type of corrective emotional experience to counterbalance her earlier perceived betrayal by psychiatrists at the time she was hospitalized.

This story is upsetting in part because the psychiatric profession seems to have contributed to the patient's problems. On the other hand, it shows that even dismal presentations often offer the sort of life events and interpersonal situations on which IPT can capitalize. For a patient like Ms. L, who distrusted therapists (with some reason), IPT also may have been helpful in providing a straightforward treatment approach and an involved, openly supportive therapist.

Self-Assertion Amid Disputes

Ms. M, a 48-year-old married, tenured professor, came in having rather hopelessly diagnosed herself as having chronic depression. She described a successful academic career that had brought her little happiness; in her male-dominated department she felt ignored by her senior colleagues and taken advantage of by her juniors. She was asked to teach courses that male assistant professors did not want. Nor did she get much respect at home. Her husband of more than 20 years was verbally and occasionally physically abusive, especially when he drank. Ms. M had considered but decided against taking antidepressant medication. Her Ham-D score was 27, reflecting a depressed mood, guilt, passive suicidal ideation, early and mid-insomnia, ruminative anxiety, low energy and libido, and a pervasive sense of helplessness, hopelessness, and worthlessness.

Ms. M's therapist agreed that she was suffering from dysthymic disorder. She offered her a 16-week trial of IPT-D with a focus not only on the role transition into euthymia but also on her role disputes with her work colleagues and her husband. The therapy focused on *transgressions;* weren't her colleagues breaking the rules? Hadn't she earned a right to greater respect for her work? And wasn't this even more the case at home? Discussions in the office helped Ms. M change her perspective from a wronged victim into an avenging one. Once set on the right path, she needed little role playing to voice her feelings. She spoke up in departmental meetings and was elated to see that "my bluff worked"; people listened to her; one colleague spontaneously apologized for his past injustices. After a few weeks Ms. M no longer felt she was bluffing but that she deserved to be listened to.

With the work front more secure, the therapeutic team turned to the home front. The goal was to help Ms. M's husband stop drinking and to find a way to negotiate their differences without verbal abuse. She was not afraid of physical violence so long as he was not drinking but seemed uncertain how to shift from her passive stance at home.

> *Ms. M:* I felt this at first at the University, too, but with my husband I really don't want to make waves.

> *Therapist:* Why is confronting him so bad? You'll feel some immediate anxiety if you do, but you might solve the situation. Otherwise there's the longer discomfort of *not* addressing the situation, keeping your feelings in, and having things continue the way they have been. . . . But I understand your doubts; relationships are usually more complicated than the workplace, since there are fewer rules . . . .

The therapist helped Ms. M to define what she wanted at home; they agreed that neither she nor her husband could be happy with the current situation. They discussed alcoholism and ways of dealing with it, including Alcoholics Anonymous and Al-Anon. They considered whether it might be helpful to invite Mr. M to join the treatment for a session or two versus pursuing the unilateral strategy of individual IPT for role disputes. Ms. M raised the question of whether she should leave him. Although she decided she did not want to end the marriage, the idea that she could survive alone if she had to gave her the strength to confront her husband. He was initially taken aback by his wife's new tactics; despite her accomplishments in her academic field, neither of them seemed to have regarded her as a competent spouse. Nonetheless, he agreed to stop drinking and did so at least for the duration of the IPT treatment. As Ms. M's dysthymic disorder resolved (Ham-D = 6), her libido returned, and the sexual aspect of the marriage improved as well. Ms. M has continued to do well in monthly maintenance IPT.

CHAPTER 6
Complex Cases of Dysthymic Disorder

First begin with prayer and then use physick;
not one without the other but both together.

—Robert Burton,
Treatise on Melancholia

In this chapter, I address difficult situations that arise with dysthymic patients. I include a discussion of the choice and combination of therapies for patients who do not respond to monotherapy.

Differential Therapeutics of Dysthymic Disorder

When a dysthymic patient enters your office, what should you do? There is no single answer to this question, but the available research and my own experience in treating this syndrome offer some suggestions. Research has provided few guideposts about which dysthymic patients will respond differentially to which treatments (Kocsis et al. 1989), but patients who fail to respond to medication may respond to psychotherapy and vice versa (Markowitz 1994; see Serial Treatment Data, pp. 31–32).

129

As discussed in Chapter 2, antidepressant medication is the best proven treatment for dysthymic disorder and other forms of mood disorder. On the other hand, there is some evidence that psychotherapies such as interpersonal psychotherapy (IPT) and cognitive-behavior therapy (CBT) also may be helpful in their own right, and the combination of pharmacotherapy and focused psychotherapy may have advantages for some patients over either treatment alone.

Given our limited data on the treatment of dysthymic disorder, it is premature to construct a definitive treatment algorithm. Nonetheless, discussion of a tentative approach to sequential treatment may be helpful. For many patients, the first choice of treatment depends on patient preference (see Table 2–1). Some patients have strong beliefs that they need a medication or psychotherapy. The therapist should present the patient with an explanation of the full range of treatments, and their relative merits, untainted insofar as possible by the therapist's own ideologic beliefs and preferences about treatment.

A Treatment Algorithm[1]

Step 1: Diagnosis. As with any patient, you should take a careful psychiatric and general medical history in order to establish a formal diagnosis. If the patient meets DSM-IV criteria (American Psychiatric Association 1994) for dysthymic disorder, double depression, or chronic major depression, present this as a medical diagnosis; that is, that depression is an illness, not the patient's fault, and—despite years of demoralization and perhaps failed previous treatments—very likely treatable. Again, the therapist needs to maintain an appropriately optimistic stance.

Step 2: Treatment history. The history of previous treatments may suggest a logical intervention. Has the patient responded to medication in the past? (Were unsuccessful pharmacotherapy trials adequate in dosage and duration?) Has he or she previously found psychotherapy helpful? (In what respects was it helpful? Did the depressive symptoms improve?) Does the patient have a strong family history of mood disorder that has responded to medication? Even if the patient and you both have strong preferences for a mode of treatment, you should present all the available treatment options: medication, psychotherapy, and their combination,

---

[1] This section is adapted with permission from Markowitz JC, Kocsis JH: "The Current State of Chronic Depression." *Journal of Practical Psychiatry and Behavioral Health* 1:211–218, 1995.

explaining the likely benefits, liabilities, and evidence for the efficacy of each. It is important that the patient understand all the possibilities—their very variety should convey some hope—and that you and the patient agree on the treatment plan.

Step 3: Initial treatment intervention.   Assuming that the patient has not previously received treatment, it may be reasonable to begin with either pharmacotherapy or psychotherapy alone. Severity of symptoms in double depression or chronic major depression, or significant suicidal risk, argues for including medication in the treatment regimen.

If you start a medication trial, you may reasonably assume that most antidepressant medications—tricyclic antidepressants (TCAs), monoamine oxidase inhibitors (MAOIs), and serotonin reuptake inhibitors (SSRIs), and others—will have similar efficacy and will differ principally in their side-effect profiles. The patient should understand the tradeoffs (e.g., dry mouth, constipation, and weight gain with TCAs or MAOIs versus headaches and sexual dysfunction with SSRIs).

Do not assume that dysthymic disorder is a "mild" depression and therefore requires lower than usual doses of antidepressant medication. Dysthymic patients deserve vigorous treatment with antidepressants. For example, I build the dosage of TCAs toward 300 mg unless limited by side effects and would certainly not be satisfied with a dosage of less than 150 mg (excepting nortriptyline at therapeutic blood levels). It is unfair to the dysthymic patient to halt at a middling dosage if the patient reports less than full remission of symptoms.

If you start a psychotherapy trial, use a proven, time-limited approach such as CBT or IPT for acute treatment, using the time as leverage to keep you and the patient working hard on the problem. The goal of this acute treatment should be alleviation of the chronic mood syndrome, not an overhaul of the patient's character.

Step 4: Reassessment and alternative interventions.   If the initial treatment fails to decrease symptoms within a reasonable period of time—6–8 weeks, let us say, for pharmacotherapy, or 12–16 weeks for psychotherapy—then patient and therapist should consider alternative treatments. Has the medication been titrated to the optimal dosage? Is there an obvious problem in the direction of the psychotherapy?

If the initial intervention fails or only partially succeeds, you need to address the patient's demoralization without giving in to it yourself. If side effects have limited a medication response, emphasize that the patient was not able to have a true trial of the medication. Medication can be switched or augmented; psychotherapy can be part of that augmentation. If psychotherapy fails, an initially reluctant patient may be more willing to try antidepressant medication. Whatever the situation, it is important to emphasize that hope persists, that treatment options remain, and that you will continue to explore them with the patient.

If the initial treatment has been only partially effective, therapist and patient might agree to add an adjunctive treatment to boost the efficacy of the first. The therapist should emphasize that the patient has already made some progress but that more intensive intervention may provide synergy and a better outcome. The added treatment might be either a pharmacotherapy (e.g., adding an antidepressant medication to IPT or adding a TCA or lithium to augment an SSRI) or a psychotherapy (adding IPT to pharmacotherapy).

If the initial treatment has had little benefit, the therapist should address the patient's likely demoralization and emphasize that there is still plenty of hope:

> It's natural to feel demoralized after having put in this much work and not seeing much result. But don't despair! First of all, it's the treatment that has failed, not you. And luckily there are lots of alternatives remaining.

If the first failed treatment were a medication, the therapist should consider a different medication, a psychotherapy, or both. If the first treatment were a psychotherapy, adding medication is probably the best approach. Switching medications is usually fairly simple, but in my experience switching psychotherapies has been more difficult. The rationale for taking one medication is the same as for the next, but the rationale for each psychotherapy tends to be different. It is confusing for a depressed and demoralized patient who has been taught an interpersonal, psychodynamic, or cognitive belief system to suddenly have to "switch gears" and adopt an alternative outlook. (You might compare this cognitive dissonance to a forced religious conversion.) Even if the psychotherapeutic rationales do not directly contradict one another, it is not an easy maneuver, and many patients understandably balk.

There is a second reason for sticking with the initial psychotherapy if it has been at all helpful to the patient. This is that the addition of antidepressant medication may alleviate the dysthymic symptoms and permit a previously faltering psychotherapy to have an added effect.

Step 5: Persevering.   Repeat Step 4 as often as necessary. When treatment succeeds, the results are often dramatic. Patients often feel happier than ever before; using the momentum of this improvement, they can risk starting better relationships, seeking better career situations, and otherwise undertaking the pursuit of happiness. If you feel you are running out of options or becoming demoralized, encourage the patient to see a specialist for a consultation or second opinion. There are always options.

Step 6: Continuation and maintenance treatment. Once acute treatment succeeds, the patient will in all likelihood need maintenance therapy in which to consolidate and build upon these gains. We recommend that patients on antidepressant medication continue it for at least a year or two and perhaps for life. Some medication responders swear by their medications and refuse to part with them (Kocsis et al. 1991). Given the protection medication appears to offer, this may not be a bad idea. We advise patients who do wish to stop their medication to wait until they have developed a new, euthymic "track record": until they are no longer listening to residual negative thoughts or have gained the assertiveness and social skills they need to handle their interpersonal environment. The choice, of course, ultimately belongs to the patient.

Patients who improve in time-limited psychotherapy appear to benefit from a supportive maintenance therapy, although this need not be as intensive as the acute phase (see Chapter 8). Some patients, once euthymic, develop an interest in their childhood and their internal conflicts and request psychodynamic psychotherapy (see Chapter 7). The primary goals of treatment for dysthymic patients, however, should be to achieve remission of the depressive syndrome and then to provide prophylaxis against its return.

What to Do When Psychotherapy Is Not Going Well

Maintain optimism. Dysthymic disorder can be challenging to treat. Particularly if your experience in working with this patient population is limited, it is easy to become discouraged. In my experience, the key issue is for the therapist to maintain optimism. Then his or her persuasively optimistic view, combined with the tools IPT can provide to help the dysthymic patient rethink his or her life and to develop new social skills and confidence, are likely to carry the patient through.

Encourage activity. Is the patient talking a good game in session but not putting plans into action? The therapist should then emphasize to the patient that the gains of IPT for dysthymic disorder (IPT-D) come by doing, by changing his or her interpersonal situation. The time pressure of the therapy should help goad the patient into taking appropriate action.

Reconsider the focus.   If the therapy begins to seem unfocused or emotionally superficial, it is important to review the session; an advantage of taping sessions is that you often can identify just where things got off track. Sometimes it is necessary to rethink the focus of treatment; for example, a covert role dispute might appear to be more important than another interpersonal problem area on which patient and therapist have agreed to focus (Markowitz and Swartz 1997). In this case the therapist should present a revised case formulation for the patient's agreement.

Reconsider the treatment.   IPT-D often works, but no antidepressant therapy is a panacea. If after weeks of genuine effort it really does not seem to be working, therapist and patient may agree that another treatment might work better, just as a pharmacologist and patient might decide to switch antidepressant treatments. In neither case, however, should this change be premature or cavalier, as abandoning a treatment is likely to feel like another loss and failure to an already depressed patient.

Combining Pharmacotherapy With IPT

Because IPT espouses the medical model, there is no difficulty in combining it with antidepressant pharmacotherapy. The therapist can emphasize that medical illness is often treated with a combination of medication and behavioral interventions. For example, diabetes—another illness that, like depression, can run in families—is often controlled with diet and exercise as well as with insulin or hyperglycemic pharmacology. Similarly, hypertension, myocardial infarction, and many other medical syndromes take a two-pronged approach; medication is usefully enhanced by taking care of oneself and one's behaviors. Because the latter is just what IPT offers to help the patient do, it is usually a nice fit.

Combined Treatment Research

There have been relatively few studies of combined treatment with IPT and pharmacotherapy. There have been three, in fact, all addressing major depression rather than dysthymic disorder: one acute, one continuation, and one maintenance study. The first, a 16-week trial comparing IPT, the TCA amitriptyline, their combination, and a low-contact control condition, found both monotherapies to have superior efficacy to the control; combined IPT and amitriptyline were superior to either treatment alone (DiMascio et al. 1979; Weissman et al. 1979, 1981). The continuation study found no advantage for 8 months of combined IPT and amitriptyline over either treatment alone (Klerman et al. 1974). Nor did the 3-year maintenance study of patients at high risk for recurrence of major depression find an advantage for combined monthly IPT and daily imipramine over imipramine alone (Frank et al. 1990).

No studies have addressed the combination of IPT and pharmacotherapy for dysthymic disorder, but I have found no difficulty in combining them in my private practice (see Chapter 7). In combined treatment studies of major depression, combined therapy has never performed worse than monotherapy, although it does not always show advantages (Manning et al. 1992). IPT has been helpful to patients who present for pharmacotherapy but then come to realize that psychotherapy might be a useful addition (cf. Ms. K in Chapter 5).

Is Combined Psychotherapy/Pharmacology Optimal for Most Patients?

Ongoing pharmacotherapy is probably the surest protection against the recurrence of mood disorders (Frank et al. 1990). Psychotherapy may provide advantages that medication cannot, including new social skills and help in clarifying directions and goals in life. Shouldn't the combination be ideal?

This question has lost some of its weight in recent years. The combination of psychotherapy and pharmacotherapy may be the ideal, but the economic squeeze of managed care is pressing clinicians to provide the minimum necessary treatment, not the ideal. Even before managed care, however, economics dictated the impossibility of giving all patients combined treatment; it is just too expensive. Because many patients will respond to either psychotherapy or pharmacotherapy, the combination should be reserved for more difficult patients: those with greater severity (assuming that they have not become too anergic to benefit from psychotherapy) and those who have failed to respond to a monotherapy.

Demoralization in the Health Care System

Therapists in public mental health systems and Veterans Administration (VA) hospitals have raised the question of how to treat patients demoralized within their systems. Many are "chronic patients" both in the sense of having a chronic illness and in having an interminable but resigned role as a patient in a public clinic. Expectations are low: often both the patient's and the therapist's. Such circumstances are likely to demoralize both patient and therapist and lead to a suboptimal outcome.

Therapists may succumb to the torpor, lassitude, and overwork, the bureaucracy and the paperwork of public mental health systems. Combining therapeutic burnout with the hopelessness that dysthymic patients bring to treatment yields a fearsome situation. Therapists may unconsciously settle for periodic checks on "hopeless" patients. Dysthymic patients are sure to interpret this as confirmation that their situations truly are hopeless.

The goal of treatment should be to shake up the system, to give both halves of the therapeutic dyad new hope, interest, and optimism for a better outcome. A new pharmacotherapy may provide this opportunity as well as a psychotherapy. Because so few clinicians have practiced IPT and so few patients have received it, and because it is charged with the mystique of success, IPT-D may be a good candidate for reorienting therapist and patient to therapeutic optimism.

How does one apply time-limited therapy to chronic patients inured to the treatment system, particularly in a VA system where disabled patients expect lifetime care, where there are strong regressive pulls and secondary gain? Obviously one cannot cut off treatment to these patients when time-limited therapy ends, but one can make exposure to the time-limited, "magic" treatment a precious incentive. I suggest contracting with demoralized, dysthymic patients for a 16-week, time-limited treatment, holding out the opportunity for a less intensive continuation treatment if the acute treatment goes well. If the patient does not make use of the special intervention, he or she can return to treatment as usual.

> We've been working together for a long time and have made some progress, but you still have many symptoms of chronic depression. Luckily, there's a new approach to treating your dysthymic disorder called interpersonal psychotherapy, IPT. It's been tested in a number of research studies and found to work well in various forms of depression, and there's preliminary evidence that it may work in chronic depression as well.
>
> I can't do this for everyone, but I've been thinking that IPT might make a big difference in helping you. IPT can help you solve situations in your relationships with other people while at the same time relieving your depression. It's a 16-week treatment, and I'd expect both of us to work very hard in it for those 16 weeks; if it pays off we can keep doing it. Do you want to try?

If the patient agrees, the therapeutic ante will already have been raised. As IPT is no panacea and will not help all patients, chalking up another failure might demoralize the patient further—but how much further than he or she is already? On the other hand, giving the patient the opportunity for a fresh start might make all the difference.

CHAPTER 7
The "Postdysthymic" Patient

This is the true joy in life, the being used for a purpose
recognized by yourself as a mighty one;
the being thoroughly worn out before
you are thrown on the scrap heap;
the being a force of nature instead of a feverish
selfish little clod of ailments and grievances
complaining that the world will not devote
itself to making you happy.

—George Bernard Shaw,
Man and Superman

There is almost no literature on the psychotherapeutic treatment of dysthymic patients who have responded to antidepressant medication. What follows is my understanding of psychotherapy of the "postdysthymic" patient, based on experience working with chronically depressed patients in outpatient research and private practice (Markowitz 1991, 1994; Markowitz et al. 1992a) as well as on a survey of and extended discussions with a variety of practitioners.

This chapter is based on Markowitz JC: "Psychotherapy of the Post-Dysthymic Patient."
Journal of Psychotherapy Practice and Research 2:157–163, 1993. Used with permission.

Pharmacotherapy may be sufficient treatment for some dysthymic patients, yet many require more than medication. The chronicity of dysthymic disorder, which may stretch back to childhood, has a pervasive, erosive effect on personality. Dysthymic patients have been shown to have impaired social and occupational functioning (Cassano et al. 1990; Friedman 1993; Kocsis et al. 1988b; Stewart et al. 1988). They tend to withdraw socially, to lack self-confidence and self-assertion, to have difficulty in expressing anger and taking risks. Although they may toil diligently at work to maintain a facade of normalcy (Akiskal 1981), they hesitate to let people close to them lest this expose how depressed they feel inside and lead to an anticipated rejection. Having never learned to interact socially, suffering from low energy and poor self-image, they lack confidence in dating and the social assertiveness necessary for occupational advancement. Moreover, the dysthymic individual accepts this socially inhibited, depression-tinged stance and outlook as his or her personality.

When pharmacotherapy is successful, the formerly dysthymic patient is typically relieved of neurovegetative symptoms of depression and of cognitive symptoms such as rumination, distractibility, and poor concentration and feels far less social anxiety. In my experience, the avoidant, dependent, and masochistic traits associated with dysthymic disorder often fade (Markowitz et al. 1992a); what had appeared to be "trait" proves to have been "state" (Bronisch and Klerman 1991). Yet the chronicity of the mood disorder often leaves a residue, what Beck (Beck et al. 1979) might call a dysthymic schema; the patient does not fully abandon a chronic sense of inadequacy. He or she may no longer be globally pessimistic about the future yet may still lack confidence, self-assertion, and the ability to express anger. These difficulties are particularly likely to emerge under stress, when the patient tends to revert to old, dysthymic patterns of interpersonal interaction.

In short, dysthymic patients who respond to antidepressant medication often feel better than ever before in their lives, yet they feel disoriented, naive, naked of defenses, and unsure how to proceed in a world now very differently perceived. If, as is often true, dysthymic disorder was lifelong, the patient may never have learned the skills needed to survive euthymia. Psychotherapy can serve a crucial adjuvant function at this juncture in helping the postdysthymic patient develop his or her "true" dormant personality and latent social skills after years of submersion in depression.

Pharmacotherapy may enhance accessibility to psychotherapy (Klerman 1991). Among the positive effects of medication on psychotherapy are reduced depressive symptoms, reduced distractibility, and positive placebo effect, reducing stigma. Psychotherapy for a medication-responsive dysthymic patient may be conceptualized as a form of rehabilitation rather than primary treatment. This approach is a dysthymic variation on what Penick et al. (1991) call "diagnosis-specific psychotherapy," one of whose goals is "to help patients 'objectify' their disorders by learning to distinguish features of their mental illnesses from the more enduring characteristics of their personalities." It is not supportive therapy because, regardless of formal orientation (e.g., psychodynamic, interpersonal, cognitive), it encourages a reexamination of oneself in the new, less-clouded light of euthymia.

Patient Sample

In 1993 I reviewed treatment notes on all 12 dysthymic patients who received combined psychotherapy and pharmacotherapy in my recent private practice and who responded to initial pharmacotherapy. All met DSM-III-R (American Psychiatric Association 1987) criteria for dysthymia, primary type, early onset. Antidepressant medications included fluoxetine (range 20–40 mg qd), nortriptyline (at therapeutic blood levels), desipramine (200–300 mg qd), phenelzine (60–75 mg qd), and in one case lithium augmentation (600 mg qd) (see Table 7–1). Response was defined as the remission of depressed mood and neurovegetative symptoms (Hamilton Depression Rating Scale [Ham-D] [Hamilton 1960] score ≤ 6) for a minimum of 2 months, but in fact patients reported far longer asymptomatic periods. Psychotherapy was either psychodynamic, interpersonal (IPT; Klerman et al. 1984), or cognitive-behavior (CBT) (Beck et al. 1979) therapy, with choice of therapy depending on patient preference and my clinical judgment of a given patient's aptitude for and comfort with a given approach.

Pharmacotherapy referrals from nonpsychiatric mental health professionals accounted for an additional eight cases of DSM-III-R dysthymia (six early onset, two late). The latter patients were treated jointly by these psychotherapists and myself, for individual or group psychodynamic psychotherapy, and pharmacotherapy, respectively.

The total sample of 20 patients was predominantly female (70%), single (45% never married, 30% married, 25% divorced), and white (80%; 15% Hispanic, 5% other). They had a mean age of 35.6 ± 12.4 years and reported having been depressed for a minimum of 7 years, in most cases for essentially all of their remembered lives. The gender, age, marital status, and duration of illness are typical of dysthymic patients who present for treatment (Markowitz et al. 1992a). I had followed these patients for a mean 1.3 ± 0.6 years (range 0.6–3.0 years); some remain in treatment in 1997. The two treatment groups did not vary significantly on demographic variables.

Table 7–1. Characteristics of postdysthymic subjects and treatment

Patient	Age	Sex	Marital status	Duration of dysthymia[a]	Medication	Psychotherapy	Length (years)[b]
1	29	F	M	life	DMI	IPT	1.5
2	31	F	S	16	FLU	CBT	1.5
3	38	F	D	18	DMI	DYN	1.0
4	63	M	M	life	DMI	IPT	1.0
5	24	F	S	life	FLU	DYN	1.3
6	47	M	M	life	FLU	IPT	0.8+
7	24	M	S	life	FLU	IPT	0.6+
8	33	F	S	teens	FLU	CBT	0.9
9	26	F	M	life	FLU	DYN	3.0
10	39	F	D	life	PHE	DYN	1.5
11	21	M	S	life	DMI	IPT	0.6+
12	59	F	M	life	FLU/Li	DYN	0.9+
Split treatment							
1	54	M	D	35	FLU		2.0
2	28	F	D	life	FLU		0.8+
3	24	F	S	life	FLU		1.3
4	21	F	S	life	FLU		1.0
5	44	F	S	life	FLU		1.3
6	35	F	D	7	FLU		1.7

| 7 | 38 | F | S | life | FLU | 2.7 |
| 8 | 33 | M | M | life | FLU | 0.8 |

[a]Lifelong, or age at onset.
[b]Years of current treatment.

Note. S = single; M = married; D = divorced; DMI = desipramine; FLU = fluoxetine; Li = lithium carbonate; PHE = phenelzine; IPT = interpersonal therapy; CBT = cognitive-behavior therapy; DYN = dynamic psychotherapy.

In the cases I treated by myself, therapy began with identification of the diagnosis of dysthymic disorder and giving patients the sick role—standard maneuvers of brief therapies of depression, particularly of IPT (Klerman et al. 1984; Markowitz and Swartz 1997). Initial sessions focused on depressive symptomatology and its effects on social and occupational functioning. Once antidepressant medication took effect and symptoms waned, we were faced with differentiating what the patient had long considered his or her personality from the suddenly dislodged depressive disorder. In the eight split-treatment cases, the referring psychotherapists reported, coincident with the advent of psychopharmacology, an acceleration and focal shift in what had usually been a chronic supportive treatment: from a repetitive discussion of symptoms to a new, more exploratory emphasis on developing social skills and facing new situations. In all cases I emphasized a "medical model" to the patient: that he or she had been suffering from a chronic mood disorder, often mistakenly accepting it as a true personality or self, and that the relief afforded by medication provided an opportunity to rethink that self-image.

This approach is a sequential variant on the usual concept of combined psychotherapy/pharmacotherapy of depression as a relatively synchronous intervention. It echoes the finding of Klerman and colleagues that pharmacotherapy alleviated symptoms earlier, whereas interpersonal therapy preferentially enhanced work and social functioning later in treatment (Weissman et al. 1981). It also echoes the structure of the original IPT treatment study, which added IPT to patients who had already begun to show a response to the tricyclic antidepressant amitriptyline (Klerman et al. 1974).

Case Examples

The following case vignettes share certain commonalities in illustrating how patients remitted from dysthymic disorder began to develop self-assertion, self-esteem, appropriate risk taking, expression of anger, and greater social comfort and adjustment.

> Ms. N, a 29-year-old, remarried Hispanic mother of four, presented with lifelong depression exacerbated by the death of her alcoholic father. Sexually abused in childhood, she described her subsequent chaotic life as uniformly unhappy. She had no history of psychiatric treatment. In addition to meeting diagnostic criteria for dysthymic disorder, her emotional lability and impulsivity suggested histrionic personality disorder. She showed an immediate, dramatic, and sustained response to desipramine 250 mg qhs: within a

month her Ham-D (21-item version) score fell from 24 to under 4.

Her impulsivity also diminished markedly—she no longer seemed "histrionic"—but she now felt unsure how to proceed. In weekly interpersonal therapy she then reassessed her relationship with her husband and children, who themselves had to adjust to her vastly changed personality. With the therapist's encouragement, she began to take unprecedented, but proper, risks. She applied for a civil service job; when obstructed by a bureaucratic technicality, she applied to college, where she is currently doing well. She opened her first bank account and credit line, recognizing these as achievements of independence for a woman as helpless as she had previously felt. Approaching each new challenge raised anxieties about her adequacy, her competence to cope; each success affirmed her confidence and reduced anxieties about her next venture.

"I feel I have to make up for wasted time . . . it's like I had a terminal illness, and now I'm okay and have to make the most of it, like getting out of a prison. I always thought I was just that sad person. Gaining confidence: it's scary, but I'm taking new chances and things are going well."

A year and a half later, still testing her limits, she is beginning for the first time to experience a secure sense of herself as a euthymic individual.

Ms. O, a 26-year-old, married graduate student with lifelong dysthymic disorder, responded to fluoxetine 10–20 mg qam, and her Ham-D score dropped from 22 to 3. She initially appeared to have strong masochistic/self-defeating and avoidant traits, which faded with medication treatment. Still, she was unsure how to interact with those around her. Psychodynamic treatment, at first once and then twice weekly, helped her overcome the "wall" she put up against intimacy, first with the therapist and then with others. Two previous courses of psychotherapy had been unsuccessful, in retrospect probably because her depressive symptoms had dominated the treatment.

Therapy focused on her sense of vulnerability in relationships with others. Over time she gradually increased the risks she took in opening up to her husband, friends, and family. Her performance in school improved as she took greater risks in situations where she had previously hung back. Self-confidence markedly improved. After a year she planned a pregnancy, we tapered her medication, whereupon neurovegetative symptoms of depression returned. She was able to maintain much of her improved self-image despite and perhaps even because of this relapse, which demonstrated to her the demarcation between "self" and mood disorder. Upon resuming medication, she has remained euthymic during 3 years of combined treatment and 8 months of pure medication maintenance, functioning well and happily both in her career and as a wife and mother.

Ms. P, a 21-year-old student from a family in chronic conflict, reported life-long depression and social withdrawal. Struggling to pass courses and stung by the indifference of a fellow student whom she had viewed as a potential boyfriend, she entered psychotherapy with a psychologist. She said little over 10 months of weekly sessions and eventually agreed to a psychopharmacology consultation. On evaluation she appeared depressed, anxious, making poor eye contact, with strongly avoidant features and a certain indefinable oddness. Her Ham-D score was 21.

After showing little response to fluoxetine 20 mg over 8 weeks, she then improved dramatically on fluoxetine 40 mg po qam. In addition to the eva-nescence of depressive symptoms, she and her psychologist reported that she found new purpose in her sessions. Reviewing her diaries, Ms. P was amazed at the change in her mood and sense of self. She expressed some sadness at time lost and "wasted" and some anxiety mixed with excitement and confu-sion about dating. She took on a fuller course load than ever before and got better grades. It took experience to recognize that, although disappointments hurt, they no longer felt crushing nor heralded the return of depression. In psychotherapy she was encouraged to make efforts to date and tentatively be-gan to do so. She remains asymptomatic on fluoxetine 40 mg after 11 months of treatment.

Discussion

These cases raise issues about the nature of personality and the importance of psy-chotherapy in helping "true" personality awaken after years of submersion beneath a chronic mood disorder. Most of these patients described the sense of entering a new life, of seeing in color for the first time rather than in black and white. They could clearly distinguish between life before and after medication, suddenly recognizing that they had long been "sick" and were now "healthy." In psychotherapy they were able to reject the remains of dysthymic disorder as an ego-alien medical disorder, discovering themselves in its ashes. Although studies have shown that dysthymic pa-tients make significant gains in social functioning from 6 weeks of antidepressant medication without psychotherapy (Friedman 1993; Kocsis et al. 1988b; Stewart et al. 1988), psychotherapy remained an important adjunct for many patients in mourning their years lost and adjusting to an exciting but also potentially over-whelming new set of circumstances.

Indeed, it appeared as if pharmacotherapy offered these patients a sudden "new lease on life," which then spurred them on to greater psychotherapeutic involvement and gains. These postdysthymic patients shed not only symptoms but much of what had appeared to be character disorders. In psychotherapy they were newly malleable and motivated.

Research on psychotherapy of dysthymic disorder is sorely lacking, yet it may have utility as either a primary treatment or complementary to pharmacotherapy. The 1987 National Institute of Mental Health Workshop on Combined Medication and Psychotherapy in Depression cited dysthymic disorder as a prime diagnostic target for combined antidepressant therapies. Combined treatment is enjoying new interest, particularly in the area of affective disorders (Beitman and Klerman 1991; Frank et al. 1990). Our knowledge of the specificity of different psychotherapies does not permit differential therapeutics for dysthymia; evidence of mode specificity is limited (Sotsky et al. 1991), and treatment usually is determined more by the psychotherapist's breadth of expertise than by the patient's strengths and aptitudes. Nevertheless, our experience in working with dysthymic patients yields several therapeutic guidelines.

Psychotherapy of postdysthymia needs to help the patient recognize the influence of state on trait (Bronisch and Klerman 1991; Loranger et al. 1991): namely, the fact that what he or she has considered him- or herself has been clouded by the pall of chronic depression. Dysthymic disorder is often accompanied by comorbid axis I and II diagnoses, such as social phobia and avoidant, self-defeating, and dependent personality disorders (Markowitz et al. 1992a). Are these so-called comorbid disorders and personality traits largely expressions of dysthymic disorder itself, and do they disappear or diminish with its treatment? Bronisch and Klerman (1991) and others (Hirschfeld 1990; Hirschfeld et al. 1983; Reich et al. 1987) have noted the effect of mood on personality functioning and provided preliminary evidence that apparent personality traits may evanesce with treatment of an underlying mood disorder.

A medical model approach appears helpful, in effect giving the patient a convalescent if not a sick role (Parsons 1951). Psychotherapy of the postdysthymic patient becomes an exploratory venture to distinguish depressive residue from the emerging, long-suppressed personality. This generally involves identification of masochistic and avoidant patterns of social behavior and encouragement of appropriate expression of anger and reasonable risk taking. Mourning of lost years and opportunities is also frequently helpful. The impetus of medication response, and the gradual realization that this marvelous symptomatic improvement is going to persist, often fuel the patient's involvement in psychotherapy.

Is such psychotherapy more than simple rehabilitation? Postdysthymic patients seemed not only to learn new social skills in psychotherapy but to see themselves and those around them differently. This suggests an unexpectedly fluid development of their internal representations of self and others (i.e., of their object relations). We are now using the Inventory of Interpersonal Problems (Horowitz et al. 1988) as a potentially more subtle measure to study interpersonal changes in dysthymic patients treated with medication alone, psychotherapy alone, and their combination. Findings suggest a statistically significant improvement on all six component factors (Markowitz et al. 1996). This study may elaborate and confirm our current impressions.

Limitations of these observations must be clearly stated. The discussion is based on a small, naturalistic sample of medication responders. Not all dysthymic patients respond to antidepressant medication and not all postdysthymic patients who do so want or necessarily need psychotherapy. There has been essentially no research on rehabilitative psychotherapy for recovered mood-disordered patients. While we await the results of such research, our experience suggests that psychotherapists need not fear that the benefits of pharmacotherapy will deprive them of their caseloads. And given the chronicity of symptoms and likelihood of comorbid complications, combined therapy often may be indicated for dysthymic disorder.

Addendum

I wrote the first part of this chapter in 1993. My subsequent experience with post-dysthymic patients has borne out this earlier review. Dysthymic patients who respond to medication need time and new experience to normalize their long-distorted emotional equilibrium. Some patients respond quickly to medication but may take years to adjust psychologically. Psychotherapy, even of relatively infrequent dosage, may help some of these patients to investigate and reinforce their appropriate range of feelings. My approach to working with these patients has increasingly shifted to an IPT model because that so directly connects feelings with current life experience. The key issues by now should be familiar to the reader.

One is for the patient to learn *appropriate self-assertion, expression of anger, and risk taking.* Another is to learn to *distinguish appropriate emotional responses from depression:* for example, to emotionally understand the difference between normal sadness when something painful occurs and disproportionate depression. I encourage formerly dysthymic patients to recognize once-feared emotions, now uncontaminated by depression, as useful reactions to their environment; sadness, anxiety, and anger all reflect understandable and potentially helpful responses to interpersonal events.

One patient finally came around to the idea that she had been suffering from a medical illness:

> You know, this really must be a somatic illness, to change so much with just a pill . . . .

Mr. Q, a 41-year-old, married college professor, reported a lifelong depression marked by a tendency to irritable outbursts. Years of psychodynamic psychotherapy with a sympathetic therapist had given him insight and preserved his marriage to a difficult, depressed wife. A trial of paroxetine 20 mg po qd produced almost overnight relief of depressive symptoms and a significant diminution in his anger. He had "never felt like this before" and was (for the first time in his life!) overjoyed.

Because the patient had initially continued to see his psychotherapist, my psychological interventions as his pharmacologist consisted mainly of psychoeducation about dysthymic disorder as a medical illness and an encouragement to take social risks to achieve his wishes and to test out his newfound, nondepressed self. He soon left psychotherapy, left his college, and left his wife. I saw him only every few months for medication visits; he said he had had enough of psychotherapy and could not afford more treatment. After some experimentation with other relationships he returned to his wife, negotiating a more balanced relationship than they had previously had, and pressing her to get treatment for her own depression. He also found a new, more satisfying career path.

Once he had left his psychotherapy, I felt freer in pursuing an interpersonal approach in our irregular visits. We described his response to medication as the onset of a continuing role transition in which he could discover his new potential. This included pursuing fantasied sexual relationships with women—rather than telephone and computer sex, as in the past—and finding himself to be a more competent lover than he had previously believed. These success experiences and the increased self-esteem they brought facilitated his return to his wife and altered the rather masochistic role he had had in their marriage.

Even 2½ years after his medication-induced euthymia, Mr. Q continued to report new discoveries of feeling and potential. At a recent visit we discussed his discomfort with feeling grief after several relations and a beloved pet had died. Although we had previously discussed the difference between mourning and melancholia, it took the presence of actual grief to help him address his fears that these feelings represented a return of his dysthymic disorder. Yet his self-esteem was stable, he did not blame himself, and sleep was disrupted for only a day or two. We discussed his feelings of loss as *normal, useful signals in response to environmental events* and the importance of his accepting rather than hiding from these feelings as part of his continuing, healthy adjustment to euthymia.

Other Personality Disorders

A robust medication response reassures the therapist about the state/trait issue; removing the mood disorder should help disentangle what is personality and what has simply been the result of depression. Some dysthymic patients I have treated have not had the typical avoidant, dependent, or self-defeating features (see Chapter 1). Rather, they have compensated for their inner depressive feelings by sealing them off beneath a veneer of aggressive social confidence. This typically allows them to function well in a business role (e.g., in sales) but essentially precludes emotional intimacy. Medication may remove the underlying mood disorder while leaving the patient with a constricted and unhelpful social repertoire.

Another way of looking at this is that in some instances dysthymic disorder can erode personality or prevent its development, leaving the patient with a pseudoavoidant, dependent, borderline, or self-defeating personality disorder (i.e., symptoms in the "C" [anxious] cluster of the DSM-IV axis II personality disorder spectrum). These apparent traits are likely to improve greatly with antidepressant medication or psychotherapy, although the patient may need some rehabilitation and reorientation to develop new skills. In other cases dysthymic disorder may be incidentally comorbid with an axis II disorder, often in cluster "B" (dramatic) or occasionally in cluster "A" (paranoid, schizoid, schizotypal). In such cases the personality traits are not necessarily depressively tinged, and the therapist's work is probably harder.

Ms. R, a 44-year-old, divorced white Catholic self-made businesswoman, reported lifelong dysthymic disorder but covered it with an assertive, competitive, voluble facade. She reported having been the "strong one" growing up with a depressed mother and sister. She did not finish college because of an early, brief, and disastrous marriage—evidently an attempt to escape her home. She was ashamed of lacking a diploma, which she considered a terrible secret, concealed on her resume and from all her friends. Nonetheless, her strong, smart, polished, attractive, and aggressive presentation helped her succeed in business.

Her relationships with men were many but brief. She met them easily but came across as so powerful that she intimidated most; the others, seeing through to her evident discomfort, tended to take advantage of her. She invariably got involved with men who belatedly revealed they were married. Others borrowed money from her that they never repaid. Those who were gentle, sympathetic, or warm she tended to view as weak, easy catches not worth the sport.

Ms. R had spent 8 months in a weekly psychodynamic psychotherapy but hated to describe the painful events of her past or to examine painful emotions. She therefore sought antidepressant medication and responded impressively to fluoxetine 20 mg. She felt much better, her sleep and concentration improved and her anxiety decreased. She immediately discontinued the psychotherapy and for some 5 years seemed content with quarterly pharmacotherapy maintenance visits. Symptomatically she continued to do well but had ongoing difficulties at work and in romantic relationships. She claimed that she "wanted to be taken care of," but her aggressive interactions tended to scare away caring men. She was quick to dismiss men who did not meet exacting material and social qualifications, but she neglected their emotional qualities and so tended to meet "creeps" who took sexual or material advantage of her and then left. In sum, she seemed to have characteristics consistent with narcissistic and histrionic personality disorders—or, as is typical in DSM-IV, personality disorder not otherwise specified.

The death of her father, some business reversals, loneliness as she saw her friends marry, and an unhappy 44th birthday brought her in for a medication session. Usually extremely well groomed, she was dressed in running sweats, without her usual makeup. It was at this session that she made the grim confession about not having a college diploma ("I've never told this to a living soul except my mother and sister"). We discussed her unhappiness, which had not responded to gradual increases in fluoxetine to 30 mg and then 40 mg qd. She had no neurovegetative symptoms of depression but was miserable about her life. She did not want to deal with the past but liked the idea of IPT for dysthymic disorder as a more structured, goal-oriented, and future-oriented approach than her previous therapy.

Within a time-limited framework we focused on her feelings about her father's death (complicated bereavement) but principally on the role transition accompanying the improvement of her dysthymic disorder. Now that the medication had helped her, I asked, was it safe to let her guard down and risk emotional vulnerability? She said she would try and did. Sessions focused on her interactions with men, how she felt and what she wanted in these interactions (she was not given to reflection), and what options she had to achieve what she wanted.

A key event was her accepting a date with Paul from the outer boroughs of New York City—she usually dealt only with Upper East Side Manhattanites.

Intensive focus on her attitudes about Paul's occupation, attitudes, and social status helped her anticipate her responses in this dating situation and to change some of them. She also struggled to "let down her guard," trying to risk talking about her feelings. Ms. R and Paul continued to date, providing a laboratory for her interpersonal skills that she could work on in sessions. Her mood, outlook, and social life improved immeasurably. Aspects of her previous personality remained, but her social skills were better and she seemed aware of what had been a critical blind spot in her interpersonal functioning.

With characterologically disordered patients, the development of a therapeutic alliance takes on even greater importance than usual. A secure therapeutic alliance is a necessary foundation from which to gently press the patient to alter long-standing behaviors. With hard work, it is possible to build a strong alliance even with many patients who have significant characterological difficulties. Once this groundwork is established, the usual business of IPT can proceed.

Postdysthymic patients are easier to treat in psychotherapy than are dysthymic patients because their mood symptoms have largely responded to antidepressant medication. They do present the challenge of helping the patient to recognize what he or she can and does accomplish on top of the medication; many patients tend to credit their achievements while euthymic to their medication. It is important for the therapist to underscore that the patient has taken the initiative, taken the risk, and earned the victory on his or her own. The medication only protects against the relapse or recurrence of dysthymic disorder. Medication prevents the bottom from falling out, but it is the patient who then changes his or her own life.

Many postdysthymic patients also need to come to terms with how much of their life has been lost to depression. They are delighted by their new capabilities but appalled that they have been living so long under the cloud of a devastating, unrecognized, but treatable illness. They may mourn lost productivity, lost youth, and lost opportunity even as they achieve new goals in the present. They may feel angry that their doctors, or they themselves, did not sooner diagnose their condition as dysthymic disorder. (In some cases it is helpful to remind patients that the concept dates only to 1980 and has long been misunderstood.) As in any role transition, the patient must not only come to grips with the exciting potentials of the euthymic, postdysthymic role but also mourn the wasted potentials and limitations of the dysthymic past.

CHAPTER 8
How Long Is Long Enough?

Begin at the beginning. . .
and go on till you come to the end:
then stop.

—Lewis Carroll,
Alice's Adventures in Wonderland

We do not yet have data on the risk of relapse after interpersonal psychotherapy for dysthymic disorder (IPT-D), but the chronicity of dysthymic disorder and the effectiveness of monthly IPT maintenance for patients with recurrent major depression (Frank et al. 1990) leads us to consider that ongoing treatment is advisable. Monthly sessions have been sufficient to preserve euthymia for several IPT-D pilot patients who now have 2 and more years of follow-up. We accordingly offer subjects who respond to IPT-D monthly ongoing treatments for at least 6 months (the continuation phase) and, with the patient's agreement, up to 2 years and more (maintenance).

For major depression, relapse has been defined as occurring in less than 6 months after remission, whereas recurrence is somewhat arbitrarily defined as greater than 6 months (Frank et al. 1991b). We know far less about the course of dysthymic disorder; perhaps the concept or time frame of relapse and recurrence should differ for this chronic illness. In any case, the limited pharmacotherapy data indicate that relapse is likely when medication is stopped after 6 months (Kocsis et al. 1996).

Our pilot data followed the precedent of Frank et al. (1989, 1990) in offering

151

monthly continuation and maintenance sessions. Yet this is a new and open area for study. The current study we are conducting entertains various continuation strategies in an effort to determine which are most efficacious for dysthymic patients.

Continuation sessions follow much the same format as acute treatment sessions. Therapists begin sessions by asking, "How have you been in the past month?" and proceed as before by linking affect to interim events. Continuity with material from acute treatment should be maintained by pursuing themes that remind the patient of the earlier work and problem area. For example: What is the state of the previously troubled marriage? How is the patient using the new options previously explored? Are there new wrinkles in the old situation? Is the role transition proceeding as planned? As in the acute treatment, it is important to seek out specific examples from the interval since the last session.

The therapist should remark upon persistence of symptom remission as evidence that the patient has indeed made significant changes in his or her life and mood disorder. An often helpful observation is that it takes time, after years of dysthymia, to believe that it really has receded. The patient may need some time to develop a new, undepressed track record in euthymic life to counter chronic pessimism.

In continuation and maintenance treatment the IPT-D therapist may be most important as a stable object and resource, providing monthly reassurance that the shakily euthymic patient has not been abandoned. This persisting presence in the background of the patient's interpersonal environment often seems more important than the content discussed in continuation sessions; the patient usually has learned the method and needs relatively little reinforcement. Sometimes the same lesson does need to be reworked in more than one situation, a sort of interpersonal "working through." But the reminder that the patient has an illness often *does* seem helpful; it takes dysthymic patients a while to integrate a new, euthymic identity and to see the past as having been colored by illness.

It also may be important to maintain a clear interpersonal focus to give ongoing form and structure to the therapy; the Pittsburgh maintenance IPT study showed that therapists and patients who maintained a focus on interpersonal themes had a better outcome than those who did not (Frank et al. 1991a).

The continuation and maintenance phases often provide opportunities for patients to "normalize" emotions: that is, to learn to experience formerly feared reactions such as sadness, anger, and anxiety as useful social responses rather than symptoms of depression. It is a signal victory when a formerly dysthymic patient comes in after a significant other has died and reports proudly: "I'm sad, but I'm not depressed."

How Long Is Long Enough?

We do not really know the answer, even for medication, where 6 months of treatment is not long enough for most dysthymic patients. Patients often vote with their feet on the need for treatment. Some want the security of ongoing treatment and if anything need to be pushed to greater independence. Others, not liking the idea of treatment that may potentially be lifelong, stop treatment and return only if their symptoms do. Some patients like gradually to reduce the frequency of sessions, moving from monthly to bi-monthly, later to seasonal or yearly visits rather than terminating altogether.

I have had patients do well for a number of years and then return surprised and disappointed by a recurrence. In such cases it is important to present the medical model:

> This is a recurrent illness, not your fault; but now let's see what we can do about this new episode.

The more the patient can build confidence in his or her social skills, and the more the patient can optimize his or her interpersonal situation, the less should be the chances of recurrence. I believe that this is usually the case, but biological vulnerability may override these other factors. I have seen patients return to treatment saying,

> You know, I really know better, I think I'm doing everything right, and yet the symptoms are coming back anyway. I'm fighting them, but they're coming back anyway.

And I've agreed with them. Often they respond to a few "refresher" sessions of IPT, to an antidepressant medication, or both. For patients whose dysthymic disorder recurs, my tendency is to suggest antidepressant medication as the surer prophylaxis against further relapse or recurrence. I present this as the better proven treatment—there have been controlled maintenance studies of pharmacotherapy but not of psychotherapy for dysthymic disorder.

Thus while its time limit is an important element of acute IPT, and the time frame should be renegotiated in each subsequent phase (continuation, maintenance), for dysthymic patients the duration and end point of maintenance therapy is unclear. It is important to help a patient build a sense of independence, but it may be helpful for the therapist to remain available in the background for a time that will likely vary from patient to patient.

CHAPTER 9
For Families and Significant Others

A life is beautiful and ideal or the reverse,
only when we have taken into our consideration
the social as well as the family relationship.

—Havelock Ellis,
Little Essays of Love and Virtue

The strongest of all warriors are these two—
Time and Patience.

—Leo Tolstoi,
War and Peace

Public attitudes toward psychiatric disorders are gradually changing. Stigma in the United States probably has declined in the past decades for several reasons. Psychiatric research has made the field more of a science; research has defined psychiatric disorders reliably and produced reliable, tested treatments. Medications such as Prozac (fluoxetine) have caught the attention of the media, the public, and nonpsychiatric physicians as safe, effective

---

This chapter and appendixes 1 and 2 are intended as psychoeducation for patients and their families. Clinicians treating dysthymic patients may want to distribute copies of parts of this section to the patients or significant others.

treatments. Organizations such as the American Psychiatric Association, American Psychological Association, National Association of Social Workers, and American Nursing Association have collaborated with the U.S. Congress to make annual commemorative events such as Mental Illness Awareness Week and National Depression Screening Day educational for the public at large.

Probably still more important have been patient advocacy organizations such as the National Alliance for the Mentally Ill (NAMI) and the National Depression and Manic Depression Association (NDMDA). Whereas doctors and other mental health professionals can seem self-serving in taking political stands, patients and their families do not. Patient advocacy organizations like the National Alliance for Research on Schizophrenia and Affective Disorders have raised millions of dollars for psychiatric research. NAMI, NDMDA, and related organizations have spread across the country, fighting stereotypes of mental illness in the media and lobbying legislators for better funding and better treatment conditions.

Celebrity spokespeople have also helped. A number of prominent Americans, including William Styron, Rod Steiger, Dick Cavett, Ann Margaret, and New York Mets pitcher Pete Harnisch have acknowledged being depressed and having been helped by treatment.

One measure of how greatly American attitudes have changed is political. Senator Thomas Eagleton would have been considered for the 1972 Democratic Vice Presidential nomination had it not been revealed that he had received electroconvulsive therapy (ECT) for depression, news that immediately quashed his nomination. Yet by the 1990s the Governor of Florida, Lawton Chiles, was reelected despite a smear campaign about his ECT for depression. These are reassuring changes in public attitude.

Dysthymic Disorder

Although polls have shown that the American public has grown more accepting of depression as a treatable illness, most public education campaigns have focused on major depression and bipolar disorder. These more acutely severe disorders unfortunately have been emphasized to the neglect of dysthymic disorder. Dysthymic disorder is much harder for patients and their families to learn about. Its low profile means that dysthymic patients tend to see themselves as the source of blame. The relative silence surrounding dysthymic disorder thus contributes to the stigma dysthymic patients bear.

A poll conducted for NAMI of 1,004 Americans in January 1996 found that 56%

of the American public knew someone—a family member, friend, or co-worker—who had been diagnosed with a serious mental illness. Ninety percent of respondents said that "an imbalance in brain chemistry" contributes to chronic depression; 72% "believe[d] that treatment for people with chronic, long lasting depression can be successful." On the other hand, 41% of those polled believed that "a weakness in a person's character" contributed to chronic depression, in contrast to 31% who believed this true for schizophrenia (Belden and Russonello 1996).

Another poll, conducted by the National Mental Health Association in April 1996, found other disturbing attitudes about clinical depression and its treatment. More than one-half of those surveyed saw depression as a sign of weakness, not an illness. Less than one-third of the 1,166 American adults surveyed knew the physical symptoms associated with clinical depression. If depressed themselves, 54% reported that they would seek treatment from someone other than a health professional. Fifty-eight percent felt that depression could be effectively treated with counseling or psychotherapy, but only 41% recognized the utility of antidepressant medication. This survey purposely oversampled women, African Americans, and elderly individuals. They mentioned embarrassment and shame, denial, not wanting help, and lack of finances or insurance as the principal barriers to seeking treatment (Psychiatric News 1996). These polls suggest that although stigma about depression has declined, it remains a problem. Further public education, perhaps particularly about dysthymic disorder, is needed.

Dysthymic disorder is hard to live with, always for the patient and often for those around the patient (Lefley 1992). Depression may acutely evoke sympathy, but by the time it is chronic it is no fun for anyone. In fact, dysthymic disorder can be irritating to others. Although dysthymic patients generally do their best to keep their suffering hidden inside, it is hard to consistently generate enthusiasm when you feel depressed, exhausted, unmotivated, and socially uncomfortable. Families and significant others who interact with dysthymic patients should understand that the dysthymic person is not *trying* to have the symptoms and does not want to feel the way he or she does. *Nobody wants to be depressed.*

Dysthymic patients generally work too hard at not showing their pain. It helps to have social supports you can trust: someone you can confide in, someone you can cry with. In fact, we know that such social support protects against depression and probably helps people to come out of a depression (Brown and Harris 1978).

The material that follows may be helpful for both patients and those around them to read and to discuss together. With the patient's permission and involvement, it may at times be helpful for significant others to meet with a psychiatrist who can provide a medical imprimatur for dysthymic disorder as an illness.

APPENDIX 1
FOR FAMILIES OF A PERSON WHO HAS DYSTHYMIC DISORDER

A member of your family has been diagnosed as having dysthymic disorder. This is a chronic form of depressive disorder, a treatable medical illness. Dysthymic people often feel the problem is part of their personality, but the condition is better understood as a kind of depression. Antidepressant medication, psychotherapy, or their combination often help relieve the symptoms of dysthymic disorder.

What Can Families Do?

Educate yourselves about the illness.   Knowledge is power. Your whole family should know the enemy; you should all become experts on dysthymic disorder. To begin with, read and discuss among yourselves this review of information about dysthymic disorder. You also may want to read some of the books listed in the bibliographies here, such as Background Reading on Interpersonal Psychotherapy (see Chapter 3, p. 74). If the person in your family who has dysthymic disorder has no objection, it may be useful for the whole family to meet with the therapist to discuss diagnosis, prognosis, how dysthymic disorder affects your family, and what you can do to address it.

Be supportive.   Social supports help. One dysthymic patient I treated had to acknowledge her boyfriend's right to love her, and that his love helped her, even though she thought it showed poor judgment on his part to love "such a terrible person." Once her depression improved, she was even more grateful for the support she had received.

Blame the illness, not the patient.   If you feel frustrated by what's happening, you can bet that your loved one with dysthymic disorder feels worse. It can be easy to forget that all of you are dealing with a misery-inducing illness. Remind yourselves when things get rough; the illness, dysthymic disorder, is often to blame for the trouble.

Encourage your dysthymic family member to assert his or her needs and discomforts.   Talk openly and evenhandedly about feelings. Depressed individuals tend to see their positive wishes as undeserved (having a wish is selfish) and their negative feelings as uniquely bad. Discuss as a family that everyone naturally has wishes, everyone gets angry when crossed—but that it's harder for chronically depressed people to feel and to be comfortable in expressing those feelings. Anger can be helpful; it's better to know what's bothering someone than to have the problem continue undiscussed. Help your family member to talk about it.

Remember that dysthymic disorder is treatable.   Depressed people often feel helpless, hopeless, worthless, and even suicidal, and their despair can be contagious. Yet depression, including dysthymic disorder, is quite treatable. Sometimes treatment is easily accomplished. In other cases it may take several trials of medication, or of combinations of medications, or of psychotherapy, or of psychotherapy and medication combined. But the odds of success are much better than they appear to the depressed person. I tell patients and their families that I *like* to see depression because we're good at treating it. Other psychiatric conditions can be considerably tougher.

Join support and advocacy groups.   Get involved by contacting patient advocacy organizations on depression (listed on p. 162). There is probably an organization in your area that holds regular support group meetings. This can not only be educational but also can provide the whole family with support. Just as the dysthymic person feels uniquely alone, but is not, so can families be hurt by dysthymic disorder. Finding out that other families suffer the same kinds of illness, and learning how they cope, can provide your family with useful support and boost your morale.

APPENDIX 2
Patient Educational Materials: Dysthymic Disorder

Your doctor has determined that you suffer from dysthymic disorder, a common form of chronic depression for which effective treatments exist. (You probably won't fully believe this until you've gotten better and perhaps even some time after that.)

Dysthymic disorder means:

1. **You've been depressed for at least 2 years.** Many dysthymic people report having been depressed for as long as they can remember. You feel depressed most days and never have more than about 2 months of feeling okay—often it's rare to feel okay for more than a day.
2. **Not only is your mood low: you also have low energy, low self-esteem, and/or other symptoms.** Most chronically depressed people feel helpless, hopeless, and worthless.
3. **Your mood has probably made it harder to assert yourself or feel comfortable around other people.** When things go wrong, it feels like your fault. If you do something right, it feels like a fluke, or you feel like a fraud.
4. **It's probably hard for you to know what's your own, nondepressed personality, and what's the depression.** This is a natural consequence of having a chronic illness. In your treatment, it will be important to figure out what's you and what has been the depression.

Treatment.   Chronic depression is a medical illness that often responds to antidepressant medications and/or to psychotherapy. *THERE IS HOPE!*

Medication is the best proven treatment for this disorder.

■   There are about 20 different antidepressant medications, most of which appear
     to be equally effective; they differ in their potential side effects.
■   Medication can take several weeks to work. Although you may not believe it
     until it happens, you have about a 50% chance of getting significantly better
     with the first medication you try.
■   Side effects of the medication generally appear before benefits do, but they
     also tend to fade out, whereas benefits last.
■   If one medication doesn't work, another medication or combination of medi-
     cations may still help you. You should discuss the choices with your doctor.

Psychotherapy.   Psychotherapy is less proven as a treatment of chronic depression but may have real benefit. Interpersonal psychotherapy (IPT) and cognitive-
behavior therapy (CBT) are relatively brief treatments that have been specifically
designed to treat depression. They have been shown in careful research studies to
work with various kinds of depression.

Medication and psychotherapy for depression may be combined.
Sometimes both treatments together work better than either alone.

You may want to join a patient advocacy and support group such as the National Depression and Manic Depression Association (NDMDA) or the National Alliance for the Mentally Ill (NAMI). For more information about depression, contact

National Alliance for the Mentally Ill
200 N. Glebe Road, Suite 1015
Arlington, VA 22203-3754
Telephone: (800) 950-NAMI

National Foundation for Depressive Illness
P.O. Box 2257
New York, NY 10116
Telephone: (800) 248-4344

APPENDIX 3
Rating Scales for Therapists

IPT Problem Area Rating Scale (IPARS)

Rater: _____   Date:_____

Tape #:_____

Mark whether each problem area is present or absent, and check ALL appropriate explanatory items. At the end you will be asked to choose a primary focus for IPT with this subject based on the information available from the tape

A. Interpersonal Problem Areas

1. **Grief**   Present ☐   Absent ☐

   Uncomplicated ☐   Complicated ☐

   If grief is present, identify

   a. Deceased _____

   b. Relationship to subject _____

   c. Date of death _____

   d. Number of months between death and onset of depression _____

2. **Interpersonal dispute**   Present ☐   Absent ☐

   If present, identify:

   a. Significant other _____

   b. Does an impasse exist?   Yes ☐   No ☐

   c. Predominant theme of dispute:

      i. Authority/dominance ____

      ii. Dependence ____

      iii. Sexual issue ____

      iv. Child rearing ____

      v. Getting married/separated ____

      vi. Transgression ____

   d. Which theme checked in "c" is primary? _____

   Approximate duration of dispute in months _____

163

3. **Role transition**   Present ☐   Absent ☐

If present, identify:

   a. Diagnosis of dysthymic disorder as role transition ____

   b. Geographic move ____

   c. Marriage/cohabitation ____

   d. Separation/divorce ____

   e. Graduation/new job ____

   f. Loss of job/retirement ____

   g. Health issue ____

   h. Other (specify): _____

If more than one checked, which predominates? _____

Number of months between event and onset of depression_____

4. **Interpersonal deficit**   Present ☐   Absent ☐

If present, specify characteristics:

   a. Avoidant ____

   b. Dependent ____

   c. Masochistic ____

   d. Borderline ____

   e. Schizoid ____

   f. Paranoid ____

   g. Lacks social skills ____

   h. Other (specify): _____

If more than one checked, which predominates? _____

B. Formulation of therapeutic task

1. Rank interpersonal problem areas marked as "present" in order of their apparent impact on the subject's mood (1 = most important, 2 = secondary importance, 3 = less important):

Grief ____   Transition ____   Deficit ____   Dispute ____

2. Which problem areas would you use to formulate a treatment contract with the subject? (List up to 2, ranking 1 = most important)

Grief ____   Dispute ____   Transition ____   Deficit ____

3. What is the rationale for your answer to question 2? _____

_____

4. Did the interviewer on the videotape bias your response   Yes ☐   No ☐
   by indicating his/her opinion of problem areas?

5. Did the videotape provide information adequate to   Yes ❑   No ❑
   formulate a problem area diagnosis?

6. Other comments

For scoring only:

_____

_____

_____

_____

_____

Interpersonal Psychotherapy Outcome Scale—
Therapist Version

Therapist _____   Patient _____

                                      # _____

Date _____   Treatment phase
                         completed   ___ Acute   ___ Continuation

To be completed at the end of the treatment phase:

1. The primary focus of this treatment was (check one):

___ Grief (complicated bereavement)   ___ Role transition

___ Role dispute   ___ Interpersonal deficits

2. Secondary foci of treatment (check all addressed):

___ Grief (complicated bereavement)   ___ Role transition

___ Role dispute   ___ Interpersonal deficits

3. Regardless of the outcome of depressive *symptoms*, how much did the interpersonal problem area(s) change during the course of the treatment phase? Circle one number for each relevant treated problem area:

	Worsened significantly	Worsened slightly	No change	Improved slightly	Improved greatly
Grief	1	2	3	4	5
Role dispute	1	2	3	4	5
Role transition	1	2	3	4	5
Deficits	1	2	3	4	5

Describe changes:_____

_____

_____

_____

_____

_____

LITERATURE Cited

Akiskal HS: Subaffective disorders: dysthymic, cyclothymic and bipolar II disorders in the "borderline" realm. Psychiatr Clin North Am 4:25–46, 1981

Akiskal HS: Dysthymic disorder: psychopathology of proposed chronic depressive subtypes. Am J Psychiatry 140:11–20, 1983

Akiskal HS: Towards a definition of dysthymia: boundaries with personality and mood disorders, in Dysthymic Disorder. Edited by Burton SW, Akiskal HS. London, Gaskell, 1990

Akiskal HS, Rosenthal TL, Haykal RF, et al: Characterological depressions: clinical and sleep EEG findings separating "subaffective dysthymias" from "character spectrum disorders." Arch Gen Psychiatry 37:777–783, 1980

Akiskal HS, King D, Rosenthal TL, et al: Chronic depressions: part 1—clinical and familial characteristics in 137 probands. J Affective Disord 3:297–315, 1981

Altshuler KZ: Whatever happened to intensive psychotherapy? Am J Psychiatry 147:428–430, 1990

American Psychiatric Association: Diagnostic and Statistical Manual of Mental Disorders, Third Edition. Washington, DC, American Psychiatric Association, 1980

American Psychiatric Association: Diagnostic and Statistical Manual of Mental Disorders, Third Edition, Revised. Washington, DC, American Psychiatric Association, 1987

American Psychiatric Association: Diagnostic and Statistical Manual of Mental Disorders, Fourth Edition. Washington, DC, American Psychiatric Association, 1994

Angus L, Gillies LA: Counseling the borderline client: an interpersonal approach. Canadian Journal of Counselling/Revue Canadienne de Counseling 28:69–82, 1994

Arieti S, Bemporad J: Severe and Mild Depressions. New York, Basic Books, 1978

Bakish D, Lapierre YD, Weinstein R, et al: Ritanserin, imipramine and placebo in the treatment of dysthymic disorder. J Clin Psychopharmacol 13:409–414, 1993

Beck AT: Depression Inventory. Philadelphia, PA, Center for Cognitive Therapy, 1978

Beck AT, Rush AJ, Shaw BF, et al: Cognitive Therapy of Depression. New York, Guilford, 1979

Becker RE, Heimberg RG, Bellack AS: Social Skills Training Treatment for Depression. New York, Pergamon, 1987

Beitman BD, Klerman GL (eds): Integrating Pharmacotherapy and Psychotherapy. Washington, DC, American Psychiatric Press, 1991

Belden, Russonello: Summary of highlights from a national public opinion survey of Americans' awareness and attitudes regarding serious brain disorders. Presented at a news conference, Washington, DC, February 1, 1996

Bemporad J: Psychotherapy of the depressive character. J Am Acad Psychoanal 4:347–372, 1976

Bersani G, Pozzi F, Marini S, et al: 5-HT$_2$ receptor antagonism in dysthymic disorder: a double-blind placebo controlled study with ritanserin. Acta Psychiatr Scand 83:244–248, 1991

Bronisch T, Klerman GL: The current status of neurotic depression as a diagnostic category. Psychiatr Dev 4:245–275, 1988

Bronisch T, Klerman GL: Personality functioning: change and stability in relationship to symptoms and psychopathology. Journal of Personality Disorders 5:307–317, 1991

Brown GW, Harris TO: Social Origins of Depression: A Study of Psychiatric Disorder in Women. London, Tavistock, 1978

Burton R: The Anatomy of Melancholy (1621). Edited by Dell F, Jordan-Smith P. New York, Tudor, 1948

Burton SW, Akiskal HS (eds): Dysthymic Disorder. London, Gaskell, 1990

Carroll KM, Rounsaville BJ, Gawin FH: A comparative trial of psychotherapies for ambulatory cocaine abusers: relapse prevention and interpersonal psychotherapy. Am J Drug Alcohol Abuse 17:229–247, 1991

Cassano GB, Perugi G, Maremmani I, et al: Social adjustment in dysthymia, in Dysthymic Disorder. Edited by Burton SW, Akiskal HS. London, Gaskell, 1990

Charney DS, Nelson JC, Quinlan DM: Personality traits and disorder in depression. Am J Psychiatry 138:1601–1604, 1981

Chevron E, Rounsaville BJ: Evaluating the clinical skills of psychotherapists: a comparison of techniques. Arch Gen Psychiatry 40:1129–1132, 1983

Chevron E, Rounsaville BJ, Rothblum E, et al: Selecting psychotherapists to participate in psychotherapy outcome studies: relationship between psychotherapist characteristics and assessment of clinical skills. J Nerv Ment Dis 171:348–353, 1983

Chodoff P: The depressive personality: a critical review. Arch Gen Psychiatry 25:666–673, 1972

Cohen MB, Baker G, Cohen RA, et al: An intensive study of twelve cases of manic-depressive psychosis. Psychiatry 17:103–137, 1954

Cooper AM: Will neurobiology influence psychoanalysis? Am J Psychiatry 142:1395–1402, 1985

Coyne JC: Depression and the response of others. J Abnorm Psychol 85:186–193, 1976 de Jong R, Treiber R, Henrich G: Effectiveness of two psychological treatments for inpatients with severe and chronic depressions. Cognitive Therapy and Research 10:645–663, 1986

DiMascio A, Weissman MM, Prusoff BA, et al: Differential symptom reduction by drugs and psychotherapy in acute depression. Arch Gen Psychiatry 36:1450–1456, 1979

Elkin I, Shea MT, Watkins JT, et al: National Institute of Mental Health treatment of depression collaborative research program: general effectiveness of treatments. Arch Gen Psychiatry 46:971–982, 1989

Fairburn CG, Jones R, Peveler RC, et al: Three psychological treatments for bulimia nervosa: a comparative trial. Arch Gen Psychiatry 48:463–469, 1991

Fairburn CG, Jones R, Peveler RC, et al: Psychotherapy and bulimia nervosa: longer-term effects of interpersonal psychotherapy, behavior therapy, and cognitive behavior therapy. Arch Gen Psychiatry 50:419–428, 1993

Fawcett J, Epstein P, Fiester SJ, et al: Clinical management-imipramine/placebo administration manual. NIMH Treatment of Depression Collaborative Research Program. Psychopharmacol Bull 23:309–324, 1987

Fennell MJV, Teasdale JD: Cognitive therapy with chronic, drug-refractory depressed outpatients: a note of caution. Cognitive Therapy and Research 6:455–460, 1982

Frances A, Clarkin JF, Perry S: Differential Therapeutics in Psychiatry: The Art and Science of Treatment Selection. New York, Brunner/Mazel, 1984

Frank E, Kupfer DJ, Perel JM: Early recurrence in unipolar depression. Arch Gen Psychiatry 46:397–400, 1989

Frank E, Kupfer DJ, Perel JM, et al: Three-year outcomes for maintenance therapies in recurrent depression. Arch Gen Psychiatry 47:1093–1099, 1990

Frank E, Kupfer DJ, Wagner EF, et al: Efficacy of interpersonal psychotherapy as a maintenance treatment of recurrent depression. Arch Gen Psychiatry 48:1053–1059, 1991a

Frank E, Prien RF, Jarrett RB, et al: Conceptualization and rationale for consensus definitions of terms in major depressive disorder. Arch Gen Psychiatry 48:851–855, 1991b

Frank J: Therapeutic factors in psychotherapy. Am J Psychother 25:350–361, 1971

Freud S: Mourning and melancholia, in Standard Edition of the Complete Psychological Works of Sigmund Freud, Vol 14. London, Hogarth Press, 1917

Friedman RA: Social impairment in dysthymia. Psychiatric Annals 23:632–637, 1993

Goldberg DP, Bridges KW: Epidemiological observations on the concept of dysthymic disorder, in Dysthymic Disorder. Edited by Burton SW, Akiskal HS. London, Gaskell, 1990, p 104

Gonzalez LR, Lewinsohn PM, Clarke GN: Longitudinal follow-up of unipolar depressives: an investigation of predictors of relapse. J Consult Clin Psychol 53:461–469, 1985

Guelfi JD, Wiseman RL: The treatment of dysthymia with sertraline: a double-blind placebo-controlled trial in dysthymic outpatients without major depression (abstract P-2-45). Poster presented at the meeting of the European College of Neuropsychopharmacology, Venice, October 1995

Hall MJ, Arnold WN, Crosby RM: Back to basics: the importance of focus selection. Psychotherapy 27:578–584, 1990

Hamilton M: A rating scale for depression. J Neurol Neurosurg Psychiatry 25:56–62, 1960

Harpin RE, Liberman RP, Marks I, et al: Cognitive-behavior therapy for chronically depressed patients: a controlled pilot study. J Nerv Ment Dis 170:295–301, 1982

Harrison W, Rabkin J, Stewart JW, et al: Phenelzine for chronic depression: a study of continuation treatment. J Clin Psychiatry 47:346–349, 1986

Hellerstein D, Yanowitch P, Rosenthal J: A randomized double-blind study of fluoxetine versus placebo in treatment of dysthymia. Am J Psychiatry 150:1169–1175, 1993

Hirschfeld RMA: Personality and dysthymia, in Dysthymic Disorder. Edited by Burton SW, Akiskal HS. London, Gaskell, 1990, p 75

Hirschfeld R: When the Blues Won't Go Away. New York, Macmillan, 1991

Hirschfeld RMA, Klerman GL, Clayton PJ, et al: Assessing personality: effects of the depressive state on trait measurement. Am J Psychiatry 140:695–699, 1983

Hirschfeld RMA, Holzer CE III: Depressive personality disorder: clinical implications. J Clin Psychiatry 55 (suppl 4):10–17, 1994

Hooley JM, Teasdale JD: Predictors of relapse in unipolar depressives: expressed emotion, marital distress, and perceived criticism. J Abnorm Psychol 98:229–235, 1989

Horowitz LM, Rosenberg SE, Baer BA, et al: Inventory of interpersonal problems: psychometric properties and clinical applications. J Consult Clin Psychol 56:885–892, 1988

Howland RH: Pharmacotherapy of dysthymia: a review. J Clin Psychopharmacol 11:83–92, 1991

Jacobson E: Depression. New York, International Universities Press, 1971

Karasu TB, Docherty JP, Gelenberg A, et al: Practice guideline for major depressive disorder in adults. Am J Psychiatry 150 (suppl):1–26, 1993

Kaufman J: Depressive disorders in maltreated children. J Am Acad Child Adoles Psychiatry 30:257–265, 1991

Keller MB (ed): Mood disorders. Psychiatr Clin North Am 19:1–178, 1996

Keller MB, Shapiro RW: "Double depression": superimposition of acute depressive episodes on chronic depressive disorders. Am J Psychiatry 139:438–442, 1982

Keller MB, Lavori PW, Endicott J, et al: "Double depression": two-year follow-up. Am J Psychiatry 140:689–694, 1983

Keller MB, Lavori PW, Mueller TI: Time to recovery, chronicity, and levels of psychopathology in major depression: a 5-year prospective follow-up of 431 subjects. Arch Gen Psychiatry 49:809–816, 1992

Keller MB, Klein DN, Hirschfeld RMA, et al: Results of the DSM-IV mood disorders field trial. Am J Psychiatry 152:843–849, 1995

Kessler RC, McGonagle KA, Zhao S, et al: Lifetime and 12-month prevalence of DSM-III-R psychiatric disorders in the United States: results from the National Comorbidity study. Arch Gen Psychiatry 51:8–19, 1994

Klein DN: Depressive personality: reliability, validity, and relation to dysthymia. J Abnorm Psychol 99:412–421, 1990

Klein DN, Miller GA: Depressive personality in a nonclinical sample. Am J Psychiatry 150:1718–1724, 1993

Klein DN, Taylor EB, Harding K, et al: Double depression and episodic major depression: demographic, clinical, familial, personality, and socioenvironmental characteristics and short-term outcome. Am J Psychiatry 145:1226–1231, 1988

Klerman GL: Ideological conflicts in integrating pharmacotherapy and psychotherapy, in Integrating Pharmacotherapy and Psychotherapy. Edited by Beitman BD, Klerman GL. Washington, DC, American Psychiatric Press, 1991, pp 3–19

Klerman GL, Weissman MM (eds): New Applications of Interpersonal Therapy. Washington, DC, American Psychiatric Press, 1993

Klerman GL, DiMascio A, Weissman MM, et al: Treatment of depression by drugs and psychotherapy. Am J Psychiatry 131:186–191, 1974

Klerman GL, Weissman MM, Rounsaville BJ, et al: Interpersonal Psychotherapy of Depression. New York, Basic Books, 1984

Klerman GL, Weissman MM, Markowitz J, et al: Medication and psychotherapy, in Handbook of Psychotherapy and Behavior Change, 4th Edition. Edited by Bergin AE, Garfield SL. New York, Wiley, 1994, pp 734–782

Kocsis JH, Klein DN (eds): Dysthymic disorder. Psychiatric Annals 23:617–624, 1993

Kocsis JH, Klein DN (eds): Diagnosis and Treatment of Chronic Depression. New York, Guilford, 1995

Kocsis JH, Frances AJ: A critical discussion of DSM-III dysthymic disorder. Am J Psychiatry 144:1534–1542, 1987

Kocsis JH, Voss C, Mann JJ, et al: Chronic depression: demographic and clinical characteristics. Psychopharmacol Bull 22:192–195, 1986

Kocsis JH, Frances AJ, Voss C, et al: Imipramine treatment for chronic depression. Arch Gen Psychiatry 45:253–257, 1988a

Kocsis JH, Frances AJ, Voss C, et al: Imipramine and social-vocational adjustment in chronic depression. Am J Psychiatry 145:997–999, 1988b

Kocsis JH, Mason BJ, Frances AJ, et al: Prediction of response of chronic depression to imipramine. J Affective Disord 17:255–260, 1989

Kocsis JH, Markowitz JC, Prien RF: Comorbidity of dysthymic disorder, in Comorbidity in Anxiety and Mood Disorders. Edited by Maser JD, Cloninger CR. Washington, DC, American Psychiatric Press, 1990, pp 317–328

Kocsis JH, Sutton BM, Frances AJ: Long-term follow-up of chronic depression treated with imipramine. J Clin Psychiatry 52:56–59, 1991

Kocsis JH, Thase ME, Koran L, et al: Pharmacotherapy for "pure" dysthymia: sertraline vs. imipramine vs. placebo. Eur Neuropsychopharmacol 4:204, 1994

Kocsis JH, Friedman RA, Markowitz JC, et al: Maintenance therapy for chronic depression: a controlled clinical trial of desipramine. Arch Gen Psychiatry 53:769–774, 1996

Kovacs M, Feinberg TL, Crouse-Novak MA, et al: Depressive disorders in childhood; I: a longitudinal prospective study of characteristics and recovery. Arch Gen Psychiatry 41:229–237, 1984

Kramer PD: Listening to Prozac: A Psychiatrist Explores Antidepressant Drugs and the Remaking of the Self. New York, Viking, 1993

Lefley HP: The stigmatized family, in Stigma and Mental Illness. Edited by Fink PJ, Tasman A. Washington, DC, American Psychiatric Press, 1992

Lindemann E: Symptomatology and management of acute grief. Am J Psychiatry 101:141–148, 1944

Loranger AW, Lenzenweger MF, Gartner AF, et al: Trait-state artifacts and the diagnosis of personality disorders. Arch Gen Psychiatry 48:720–728, 1991

Manning DW, Markowitz JC, Frances AJ: A review of combined psychotherapy and pharmacotherapy in the treatment of depression. Journal of Psychotherapy Practice and Research 1:103–116, 1992

Marin DB, Kocsis JH, Frances AJ, et al: Desipramine for the treatment of "pure" dysthymia versus "double" depression. Am J Psychiatry 151:1079–1080, 1994

Markowitz JC: Combined therapy for a 30-year-old woman with early onset dysthymia. Hospital and Community Psychiatry 42:1103–1104, 1991

Markowitz JC: Psychotherapy of the post-dysthymic patient. Journal of Psychotherapy Practice and Research 2:157–163, 1993

Markowitz JC: Psychotherapy of dysthymia. Am J Psychiatry 151:1114–1121, 1994

Markowitz JC: Interpersonal therapy, in Core Readings in Psychiatry, An Annotated Guide to the Literature, Second Edition. Edited by Sacks MH, Sledge WH. Washington, DC, American Psychiatric Press, 1995a, pp 591–598

Markowitz JC: Teaching interpersonal psychotherapy to psychiatric residents. Academic Psychiatry 19:167–173, 1995b

Markowitz JC, Kocsis JH: The current state of chronic depression. Journal of Practical Psychiatry and Behavioral Health 1:211–218, 1995

Markowitz JC, Swartz HA: Case formulation in interpersonal psychotherapy of depression, in Handbook of Psychotherapy Case Formulation. Edited by Eels TD. New York, Guilford, 1997, pp 192–222

Markowitz JC, Moran ME, Kocsis JH: Does Psychotherapy Treat Chronic Depression? Paper presented at the 146th Annual Meeting of the American Psychiatric Association, New York, May 1990

Markowitz JC, Moran ME, Kocsis JH, et al: Prevalence and comorbidity of dysthymic disorder among psychiatric outpatients. J Affective Disord 24:63–71, 1992a

Markowitz JC, Klerman GL, Perry S: Interpersonal psychotherapy of depressed HIV-seropositive outpatients. Hosp Community Psychiatry 43:885–890, 1992b

Markowitz JC, Klerman GL, Clougherty KF, et al: Individual psychotherapies for depressed HIV-positive patients. Am J Psychiatry 152:1504–1509, 1995

Markowitz JC, Friedman RA, Miller N, et al: Interpersonal improvement in chronically depressed patients treated with desipramine. J Affective Disord 41:59–62, 1996

Mason BJ, Kocsis JH: Cornell Dysthymia Rating Scale (abstract NR231). Presented at the Annual Meeting of the American Psychiatric Association, San Francisco, CA, 1989

Mason BJ, Markowitz J, Klerman GL: IPT for dysthymic disorder, in New Applications of Interpersonal Therapy. Edited by Klerman GL, Weissman MM. Washington, DC, American Psychiatric Press, 1993a, pp 225–264

Mason BJ, Kocsis JH, Leon AC, et al: Measurement of severity and treatment response in dysthymia. Psychiatric Annals 23:625–631, 1993b

McCullough JP: Psychotherapy for dysthymia: a naturalistic study of ten patients. J Nerv Ment Dis 179:734–740, 1991

McGlashan T (ed): The Documentation of Clinical Psychotropic Drug Trial. Rockville, MD, National Institute of Mental Health, 1973

Mercier MA, Stewart JW, Quitkin FM: A pilot sequential study of cognitive therapy and pharmacotherapy of atypical depression. J Clin Psychiatry 53:166–170, 1992

Miller IW, Bishop SB, Norman WH, et al: Cognitive/behavioural therapy and pharmacotherapy with chronic, drug-refractory depressed inpatients: a note of optimism. Behavioural Psychotherapy 13:320–327, 1985

Miller IW, Norman WH, Keitner GI: Cognitive-behavioral treatment of depressed inpatients: six- and twelve-month follow-up. Am J Psychiatry 146:1274–1279, 1989

Moreau D, Mufson L, Weissman MM, et al: Interpersonal psychotherapy for adolescent depression: description of modification and preliminary application. J Am Acad Child Adolesc Psychiatry 30:642–651, 1991

Mufson L, Moreau D, Weissman MM, et al: Interpersonal Therapy for Depressed Adolescents. New York, Guilford, 1993

Parsons T: Illness and the role of the physician: a sociological perspective. Am J Orthopsychiatry 21:452–460, 1951

Paykel ES, Myers JK, Dienelt MN, et al: Life events and depression: a controlled study. Arch Gen Psychiatry 21:753–760, 1969

Penick EC, Read MR, Lauchland JS, et al: Diagnosis-specific psychotherapy, in Integrating Pharmacotherapy and Psychotherapy. Edited by Beitman BD, Klerman GL. Washington, DC, American Psychiatric Press, 1991, pp 45–68

Phillips KA, Gunderson JG, Hirschfeld RMA, et al: A review of the depressive personality. Am J Psychiatry 147:830–837, 1990

Prusoff BA, Merikangas KR, Weissman MM: Lifetime prevalence and age of onset of psychiatric disorders: recall 4 years later. J Psychiatr Res 22:107–117, 1988

Psychiatric News: Americans still harbor myths about mental illness. Psychiatric News, May 17, 1996, pp 11, 15

Reich J, Noyes R, Hirschfeld RMA, et al: State and personality in depressed and panic patients. Am J Psychiatry 141:45–51, 1987

Rockland LH: Supportive Therapy. New York, Basic Books, 1989

Rockland LH: A review of supportive psychotherapy, 1986–1992. Hosp Community Psychiatry 44:1053–1060, 1993

Rodenhauser P: Psychiatric residency programs: trends in psychotherapy supervision. Am J Psychother 46:240–249, 1992

Roose SP, Glassman AH (eds): Treatment Strategies for Refractory Depression. Washington, DC, American Psychiatric Press, 1990

Rounsaville BJ, Weissman MM, Prusoff BA, et al: Marital disputes and treatment outcome in depressed women. Compr Psychiatry 20:483–490, 1979

Rounsaville BJ, Glazer W, Wilber CH, et al: Short-term interpersonal psychotherapy in methadone-maintained opiate addicts. Arch Gen Psychiatry 40:629–636, 1983

Rounsaville BJ, Chevron ES, Weissman MM: Specification of techniques in interpersonal psychotherapy, in Psychotherapy Research: Where Are We and Where Should We Go? Edited by Williams JBW, Spitzer RL. New York, Guilford, 1984

Schneider K: Psychopathic Personalities. Springfield, IL, Thomas, 1958

Schulberg HC, Scott CP, Madonia MJ, et al: Applications of interpersonal psychotherapy to depression in primary care practice, in New Applications of Interpersonal Psychotherapy. Edited by Klerman GL, Weissman MM. Washington, DC, American Psychiatric Press, 1993, 265–291

Schulberg HC, Block MR, Madonia MJ, et al: Treating major depression in primary care practice: 8-month clinical outcomes. Arch Gen Psychiatry 53:913–919, 1996

Shea MT, Pilkonis PA, Beckham E, et al: Personality disorders and treatment outcome in the NIMH Treatment of Depression Collaborative Research Program. Am J Psychiatry 147:711–718, 1990

Shea MT, Elkin I, Imber SD, et al: Course of depressive symptoms over follow-up: findings from the National Institute of Mental Health Treatment of Depression Collaborative Research Program. Arch Gen Psychiatry 49:782–787, 1992

Simons RC: Psychoanalytic contributions to psychiatric nosology: forms of masochistic behavior. J Am Psychoanal Assoc 35:583–608, 1987

Sloane RB, Stapes FR, Schneider LS: Interpersonal therapy versus nortriptyline for depression in the elderly, in Clinical and Pharmacological Studies in Psychiatric Disorders. Edited by Burrow GD, Norman TR, et al. London, John Libbey, 1985, pp 344–346

Sotsky SM, Glass DR, Shea MT, et al: Patient predictors of response to psychotherapy and pharmacotherapy: findings in the NIMH Treatment of Depression Collaborative Research Program. Am J Psychiatry 148:997–1008, 1991

Spitzer RL, Williams JBW: Structured Clinical Interview for DSM-III-Patient Version (SCID-P, 3/1/85). New York, Biometrics Research Department, New York State Psychiatric Institute, 1985

Spitzer RL, Endicott J, Robins E: Research Diagnostic Criteria (RDC) for a Selected Group of Functional Disorders, Third Edition. New York, New York State Psychiatric Institute, Biometrics Research, 1978

Spitzer RL, Williams JBW, Gibbon M: Structured Clinical Interview for DSM-III-R—Personality Disorders (SCID-II, 10/15/86). New York, Biometrics Research Department, New York State Psychiatric Institute, 1986

Stewart JW, Quitkin FM, McGrath PJ, et al: Social functioning in chronic depression: effect of 6 weeks of antidepressant treatment. Psychiatry Res 25:213–222, 1988

Stewart JW, Mercier MA, Agosti V, et al: Imipramine is effective after unsuccessful cognitive therapy: sequential use of cognitive therapy and imipramine in depressed outpatients. J Clin Psychopharmacol 13:114–119, 1993

Stone L: Psychoanalytic observations on the pathology of depressive illness: selected spheres of ambiguity or disagreement. J Am Psychoanal Assoc 34:329–362, 1986

Stravynski A, Shahar A, Verreault R: A pilot study of the cognitive treatment of dysthymic disorder. Behavioural Psychotherapy 4:369–372, 1991

Sullivan HS: The Interpersonal Theory of Psychiatry. New York, WW Norton, 1953

Thase ME, Bowler K, Harten T: Cognitive behavior therapy of endogenous depression: part 2: preliminary findings in 16 unmedicated inpatients. Behavior Therapy 22:469–478, 1991

Thase ME, Reynolds CF, Frank E, et al: Response to cognitive-behavioral therapy in chronic depression. Journal of Psychotherapy Practice and Research 3:204–214, 1994

Thase ME, Fava M, Halbreich U, et al: A placebo-controlled, randomized clinical trial comparing sertraline and imipramine for the treatment of dysthymia. Arch Gen Psychiatry 53:777–784, 1996

Tuke S: Description of the Retreat (1813). London, Dawsons, 1964, p 152

U.S. Department of Health and Human Services: Depression in Primary Care, Vol 1: Detection and Diagnosis—Clinical Practice Guideline, No 5 (AHCPR Publ No 93-0550). Rockville, MD, U.S. Department of Health and Human Services, April, 1993a

U.S. Department of Health and Human Services: Depression in Primary Care, Vol 2: Treatment of Major Depression—Clinical Practice Guideline, No 5 (AHCPR Publ No 93-0551). Rockville, MD, U.S. Department of Health and Human Services, April, 1993b

U.S. Department of Health and Human Services: Depression in Primary Care: Detection, Diagnosis, and Treatment—Quick Reference Guide for Clinicians, No 5 (AHCPR Publ No 93-0552). Rockville, MD, U.S. Department of Health and Human Services, April, 1993c

U.S. Department of Health and Human Services: Depression Is a Treatable Illness: A Patient's Guide (AHCPR Publ No 93-0553). Rockville, MD, U.S. Department of Health and Human Services, April, 1993d

Versiani M: Pharmacotherapy of dysthymia: a controlled study of imipramine, moclobemide or placebo. Neuropsychopharmacology 10:298, 1994

Waring EM, Chamberlaine CH, McCrank EW, et al: Dysthymia: a randomized study of cognitive marital therapy and antidepressants. Can J Psychiatry 33:96–99, 1988

Weissman MM: Psychotherapy in the maintenance treatment of depression. Br J Psychiatry 165 (suppl 26):42–50, 1994

Weissman MM: Mastering Depression: A Patient's Guide to Interpersonal Psychotherapy. Albany, NY, Graywind Publications, 1995

Weissman MM, Akiskal HS: The role of psychotherapy in chronic depressions: a proposal. Compr Psychiatry 25:23–31, 1984

Weissman MM, Bothwell S: Assessment of social adjustment by patient self-report. Arch Gen Psychiatry 33:1111–1115, 1976

Weissman MM, Klerman GL: The chronic depressive in the community: underrecognized and poorly treated. Compr Psychiatry 18:523–531, 1977

Weissman MM, Markowitz JC: Interpersonal psychotherapy: current status. Arch Gen Psychiatry 51:599–606, 1994

Weissman MM, Paykel ES: The Depressed Woman: A Study of Social Relationships. Chicago, IL, University of Chicago Press, 1974

Weissman MM, Prusoff BA, DiMascio A, et al: The efficacy of drugs and psychotherapy in the treatment of acute depressive episodes. Am J Psychiatry 136:555–558, 1979

Weissman MM, Klerman GL, Prusoff BA, et al: Depressed outpatients: results one year after treatment with drugs and/or interpersonal psychotherapy. Arch Gen Psychiatry 38:52–55, 1981

Weissman MM, Rounsaville BJ, Chevron E: Training psychotherapists to participate in psychotherapy outcome studies. Am J Psychiatry 139:1442–1446, 1982

Weissman MM, Leaf PJ, Bruce ML, et al: The epidemiology of dysthymia in five communities: rates, risks, comorbidity, and treatment. Am J Psychiatry 145:815–819, 1988

Wells KB, Burnam MA, Rogers WH, et al: Course of depression for adult outpatients: results from the Medical Outcomes Study. Arch Gen Psychiatry 49:788–794, 1992

Wilfley DE, Agras WS, Telch CF, et al: Group cognitive-behavioral therapy and group interpersonal psychotherapy for the nonpurging bulimic individual: a controlled comparison. J Consult Clin Psychol 61:296–305, 1993

Zimmerman M, Pfohl B, Coryell W, et al: Diagnosing personality disorder in depressed patients: a comparison of patient and informant interviews. Arch Gen Psychiatry 45:733–737, 1988

Index

*Page numbers printed in **boldface** type refer to tables or figures.*

Blame *(continued)*
  blaming depression, 51–52, 160
  blaming interpersonal situation, 52,
    125
Bolocan, Hyam, ix
Borderline personality disorder, 14, **16,**
    22, 24, 63, 103–104, 125–126, 148,
    164
Brown, George, 112
Bulimia, **15,** 63, 123
Burton, Robert, 116

Catharsis, 57, 98, 101–102, 116
Cavett, Dick, 156
Certification of therapists, 64
Change, therapeutic, 45, 85, 90, 105, 133,
    150, **166**
Character, 4, 7, 11, 61, 65, **66,** 69, 76,
    81, 84, 87, 89, 103–105, 107, 124,
    131, 150, 157
Cheerleading, 26, 122
Cherry, Sabrina, ix
Chevron, Eve, xiv
Chiles, Lawton, 156
Clarification, 58, 111, 117
Clougherty, Kathleen, v, 65
Cognitive-behavior therapy (CBT), xiv, 7,
    22, 26, **27,** 28–32, 34, 36, 43, 50,
    62–63, 67, **68,** 69, 71, 73, 91, 95,
    110, 130–132, 139, **140–141,** 162
Cognitive-behavioral analysis system of
    psychotherapy (C-BASP), **27,** 28, 32,
    34
Columbia University College of Physicians
    and Surgeons, 31, 69, 71–72
Combined psychotherapy and
    psychopharmacology, 7, 22, 24,
    31–33, 35–36, 50, 64, **68,** 78, 82,
    96, 123–124, 129–130, 132–135,
    137, 139, **140–141,** 142–143,
    145–146, 149, 153, 159–160, 162

Communication analysis, 57–58, 106,
    117, 121–122
Comorbidity of dysthymic disorder, 14,
    15, 16, 22, 105, 145
  Axis I, 14, **15**
  Axis II, 14, **16,** 105, 148
Complicated bereavement. *See* Grief
Confidence, therapeutic, xiv, 18, 46, 62,
    64, 69–70, 72–73, 78, 85, 93–94
Confrontation, 91, 93, 106–107, 113,
    122, 127
Cooper, Arnold, ix
Cornell Dysthymia Rating Scale, 88
Cornell Psychotherapy Institute, 64
    [footnote]
Cornell University Medical College, xi, 9,
    14, 30, 32, 64–66, 90
Corrective emotional experience, 126
"Cosmetic psychopharmacology," 21

Dating, 4, 17, 101, 108, 110, 113,
    123–124, 138, 144, 149–150
Delusional disorder, **5**
Demoralization, 6, 8, 18, 82, 130–133,
    135–136
  dysthymic disorder as, 8
  of clinicians in public health services,
    135–136
  of psychotherapists facing dysthymic
    disorder, 6, 18
Dependent personality disorder, 14, **16,**
    22, 28, 105–107, 113, 138, 145, 148,
    164
Depression. *See also* Major depression,
    dysthymic disorder
  as a medical illness, xiv, 30, 33, 42, 44,
    47, 49, 51–52, 65, **66, 68,**
    72–73, 76–78, 82–84, 91–92,
    94, 108, 120, 124, 130, 134,
    142–143, 145, 147, 150–152,
    156–157, 159–160

sedative/hypnotic medication, 4, 13
"treatment resistance," 7
Phenelzine, 139, **140–141**
Pittsburgh, University of, 62, 65, 152
"Post-dysthymic" patients, 35,
137–150
Practice guidelines, 63
Preference, patient, **23,** 24, 50, 130, 133,
139, 153
Prevalence of dysthymic disorder, 12, 18,
22
Process notes, 64, 72
Process research, 46
Pseudoaltruism, 107
Psychoanalysis, 8, 22, 25–26, 41, 72
Psychodynamic psychotherapy, 4, 8, 22,
25–26, 43, 65, 67, 69, 71–73, 84,
91, 95, 120, 132–133, 139, 143, 147,
149
Psychoeducation, 47, **48,** 52, 57, **68,** 84,
86, **87,** 90, 93–96, 111, 118, 147,
155 [footnote], 155–157
Psychotherapy. *See also* Behavioral
therapy, cognitive behavioral therapy,
interpersonal psychotherapy,
psychoanalysis, psychodynamic
psychotherapy, supportive
psychotherapy, xiv, 8, 11, 23, 25–32,
34–36, 50, 81–82, 88, 93, 95–96,
120, 123, 129–134, 137–151, 153,
157, 159–160, 162
    continuation and maintenance
        treatment, 34–35, 81–82, 86,
        114–115, 123–124, 127, 133,
        135, 143, 151–153, 166
    nonspecific factors research. *See*
        Outcome research, xiv
    time limit, xiv, 7, 22–23, 26, 28, 30,
        33–34, 42, 51, 59, 62, 65, **66,**
        67, **68,** 82, 94, 131, 133, 136,
        149

Research. *See* Outcome research, process
research
Recall, 79, 161
Regression, 51, 90, 136
Rejection, fear of, 89, 108–109, 117–118,
138
Residents, psychiatric, 65, 67–73
Role disputes, 30, 45, 49, 54–55, 57, 77,
79, 82, 89, 91–92, 95, 97, 99–103,
100, 106, 111, 118, 120, 122–125,
127, 152, **163–164, 166**
Role play, xiv, 57–59, **68,** 106, 110, 112,
121–123, 126–127
Role transitions. *See also* Iatrogenic role
transition, 30, 45, 49, 54–55, 57, 60,
77, 79, 84, 89, 92, 96–97, 102–104,
103, 113, 149, 152, **164, 166**
Rounsaville, Bruce, xiv
Rush, A. John, ix

Sadness (versus depression), 97, 112, 114,
116, 143–146, 150, 152
Scarvalone, Polly, ix
Schizoid personality disorder, **16,** 56, 148,
164
Schizophrenia, **5, 15,** 157
Schizotypal personality disorder, **16,** 148
Self-assertion, 4, 12, 17, **68,** 76, 80, 101,
106–107, 109–110, 112, 120, 124,
126, 133, 138, 142, 146, 160
Self-defeating personality disorder. *See
also* Masochism, 14, **16,** 18, 22, 33,
99, 105, 110, 143, 145, 148
Self-esteem, **5,** 9, **10, 11,** 46, 55, 81, 109,
142, 147, 161
Selfishness, healthy, 107, 110
Serotonin reuptake inhibitors (SSRIs), 21,
131–132, 143–144, 147, 149
Sertraline, xi, 8, 21, 32
Sexual history, 88
Shakespeare, William, 119